SEVEN
BLACK
AMERICAN
SCIENTISTS

to my mother

SEVEN BLACK AMERICAN SCIENTISTS

ROBERT C. HAYDEN

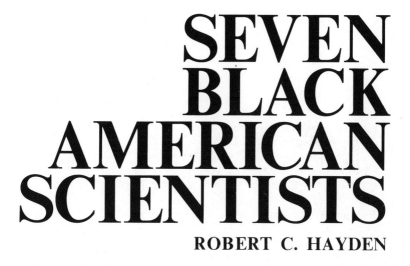

▲ ADDISON-WESLEY

§ An Addisonian Press Book

The Addison-Wesley Publishing Company, Inc.
Reading, Massachusetts 01867

Library of Congress catalog card number 77–118997
Printed in the United States of America
First printing
SBN: 201-02828-X

TABLE OF CONTENTS

FOREWORD

Black Americans have made, and are still making vital contributions to America. They have shown their skills and offered their talents in every phase of America's life and growth. Just as black Americans have made contributions to sports, literature, politics, the U.S. military, and the world of music and entertainment—they also have a record of achievement in science and technology. These achievements however, are not generally known, if known at all, by either white or black Americans.

In 1939, a committee was formed in New York City to select the most outstanding black Americans in the history of the United States. Forty-two people were chosen and their names were placed on a panel in the Hall of Fame at the New York World's Fair in 1940.

Among the list were the names of four men who had distinguished themselves in the field of natural science. They were Benjamin Banneker (1731–1806), George Washington Carver (1864–1943), Dr. Ernest E. Just (1883–1941), and Dr. Daniel Hale Williams (1856–1931). To this list of four I have added the names of three more black Americans who have also left their mark through scientific work. They are Dr. Charles R. Drew (1904–1950), Dr. Charles H. Turner (1867–1923), and Matthew A. Henson (1865–1955). This book is about their lives, the work they did, and the contributions they made to further man's mastery over nature.

One may, perhaps, ask why these seven men and their scientific works were chosen as the subject for a book. The answer lies partly in the fact that so little has been written in the past about black American scientists. And further research indicates that their contributions to knowledge are significant ones, going back a long way in our history.

In the case of the seven scientists whose biographies make up this book, information about them is generally missing from most standard science books and references. Details about them and their work in science are very scattered and difficult to obtain. Only one of them, Matthew Henson, left an autobiography to help the present-day writer of the history of science.

Being a scientist is not easy. Scientists have failures and successes as they question old beliefs and try to discover new truths. They often face the problems of getting people to give attention to their work. American scientists who are black have had the same problems as scientists who are white, plus the one of racial prejudice and discrimination.

What has it meant to be both a scientist and a black man in America?

What have been the accomplishments of black Americans in the fields of the natural sciences?

This book aims to answer these questions.

R.C.H.

Newton, Massachusetts, 1970

CHARLES R. DREW

1904–1950

Saving Lives By Saving Blood

Emergency! An ambulance races through the city streets. An automobile accident victim is rushed to a hospital. His body is bleeding from deep cuts. He is in shock. Blood, lots of it, will be needed immediately.

Once at the hospital, a nurse phones the blood bank and orders blood plasma. Within minutes several pints reach the emergency room. A doctor carefully pushes a needle into a vein in the victim's limp arm. A nurse connects a bottle of plasma to the needle with a plastic tube. The plasma begins to flow into the vein. Three more pints are given. The lost blood is being replaced. Within a few hours the victim's blood pressure begins to rise, and he comes out of shock. Another blood transfusion has helped to save a human life.

Every day in every part of the world, blood that once flowed in the blood vessels of a healthy person is put into the body of a sick or injured person. At this very moment, someone lying desperately ill on a hospital bed is receiving plasma taken from a blood donor weeks ago. This blood was preserved and stored in a blood bank until needed.

In 1940 a desperate call came from across the Atlantic Ocean. Human blood was being spilled from the wounded bodies of men fighting World War II. Soldiers in the battlefield and in hospitals lay close to death. Many lives were saved because fresh blood plasma from America was passed into the bodies of the injured men. This happened because of shipments of preserved plasma that were flown to the foreign battlefields.

It was Dr. Charles R. Drew, a black American medical scientist, who made possible the availability of stored blood plasma for blood transfusions. He did this by finding a way to preserve blood plasma for long periods of time. When the wartime need for blood arose, Dr. Drew had already set up a successful experimental blood bank to test his ideas about blood preservation. Before Dr. Drew's time there was no efficient way to store large amounts of blood for long periods of time.

BLOOD PLASMA

Everyone has seen blood ooze from a cut finger. Most people can lose about a pint of blood without suffering. If more is lost there is a danger because the body cannot replace it fast enough.

Blood is made up of a liquid part and a solid part. The two parts can be separated. If a sample of blood stands in a bottle, the solid part will settle to the bottom. This solid part consists of red blood cells and white blood cells.

The liquid part of the blood would remain on top of the piled up cells. This liquid part is called plasma. Plasma is mostly water, with dissolved calcium, sodium, potassium, iron, copper, and other elements. Plasma contains sugars, fats, and proteins. These substances are dissolved in the plasma too. Plasma also contains fibrinogen—a substance that makes blood clot when you cut yourself, hormones—substances that control different body activities, and antibodies—which help fight off disease germs. For the body to work properly, the proportion of plasma making up the blood must remain fairly constant.

Before Dr. Drew's time the breakdown of red blood cells prevented the storing of blood for more than a day or two. When red blood cells broke down, the element potassium was released into the liquid part of the blood. This change spoiled the blood and it had to be thrown away. It was very hard to get blood for transfusions, and so throwing it out was an unfortunate waste.

It was the mysteries of blood that fascinated Charles Drew when he was a student in medical school. During the time he was studying and training to be a doctor, whole fresh blood—liquid and solid parts—was being used in blood transfusions. However, he was not satisfied with the way blood was transferred from one person to another, and he was determined to do better.

DREW—THE MEDICAL STUDENT

In August, 1928, Charles Drew arrived at McGill University in Canada, to study medicine. At this time he was known for his exceptional athletic ability.

For two years before coming to McGill, Charles Drew had been the Director of Athletics at Morgan College in Baltimore, Maryland. There he had produced fine teams in football and basketball. Before his coaching job at Morgan, Drew was an outstanding college athlete and science student. At graduation ceremonies from Amherst College in Massachusetts, he was awarded a trophy as the athlete who had contributed most to athletics during his four years at college. He had starred at football, basketball, baseball, and track, just as he had during high school from 1918–1922 in Washington, D.C.

Even at McGill University, Drew's athletic achievements continued. He was elected captain of the track team and won Canadian championships in the high and low hurdles, the high jump, and the broad jump.

Charles Drew loved sports and was a tough competitor. He might have become a professional athlete or coach, but his desire to become a doctor was stronger. His ability for scholarship and achievement in medical science more than kept pace with his athletic ability.

So after five years of hard study and brilliant work, Charles Drew graduated from medical school at the top of his class. He was awarded two degrees, one in medicine, and one in surgery.

The new Dr. Drew decided to remain in Montreal to continue his learning and training in surgery. He became first an intern and then a resident doctor at Montreal General Hospital. During this period he continued to study and work 18 hours a day, just as he had done as a medical student. And things were happening in the hospital's wards and laboratories which were to help shape Dr. Drew's future.

At Montreal General Hospital, a laboratory for typing blood before transfusions had been set up. Four major blood types were known to medical scientists at the time. These were labelled, A, B, AB, and O. A person's blood type depends on the presence of certain substances on the surface of red blood cells. In general, a whole blood transfusion cannot be done unless the blood of the donor and the blood of the receiving patient are the same type.

Using just any donor for a blood transfusion can be dangerous. A person with type A blood can receive only type A blood. And a person with type B blood can receive only type B blood. A person with AB can receive blood from any of the four types. A person with type O can receive blood only from a person with type O blood. If blood types are not matched properly, red blood cells will clump together and block the flow of blood in the blood vessels. The clumping of red blood cells can cause serious illness and even death.

Dr. John Beattie, one of Dr. Drew's teachers in medical school was doing research on blood in the new blood-typing laboratory. They had become close friends during Dr. Drew's student days. Dr. Drew spent many hours in Dr. Beattie's lab—watching, learning from, and assisting his former teacher. Dr. Beattie introduced Drew to the excitement and challenge of scientific research.

Although the blood types A, B, AB, and O had been discovered in the year 1900, medical scientists were just beginning to learn about their meaning. There were still many mysteries. Dr. Drew began to read every book and article he could find on blood.

DR. DREW GIVES HIS BLOOD

As a young doctor working in the hospital's surgery division, Charles Drew saw seriously ill and injured patients die from the loss of blood. He felt that some would have lived if blood could have been given quickly enough to restore the loss. He was bothered because a patient lying on the operating room table could die if blood of the right type was not readily available.

Whenever blood transfusions were necessary, donors with a blood type like that of the patient had to be found. The laboratory was often in a turmoil. Technicians rushed madly to type the bloods of the prospective donor and receiver. Hours would pass before the blood was ready for transfusion. The time lapse could mean the difference between life and death. Often no blood donor of the right type was available. In one emergency, Dr. Drew gave blood from his own body for a man on the operating room table.

In 1935, Dr. Drew completed his residency in surgery at Montreal General, and headed home to Washington, D.C. On his mind he carried a very bothersome problem. He kept asking himself how could blood be collected, preserved, and stored for emergencies. The delays and deaths that occurred before blood transfusions could be performed distressed him. He felt that a person shouldn't die just because it took so long to obtain blood for transfusions. Blood must always be available he thought.

His research problem had been defined. Learning more about blood and how to preserve it for long periods of time was to become his main interest.

FROM TEACHER TO RESEARCHER

Back home in Washington, D.C., Dr. Drew took a teaching position at Howard University's medical school. He felt that training future black doctors was the best way he could help to advance black people in American medicine. His teaching career lasted, however, for only three years.

The Rockefeller Foundation was offering a research fellowship at New York's Columbia-Presbyterian Medical Center. Dr. Drew was offered the fellowship. He had no problem deciding to accept it since Dr. John Scudder, Research Director at the Center was doing research on blood.

So in June, 1938, Drew left Washington for New York City. The preservation and storage of blood, still a big problem in medicine, was very much on his mind. In 1937, a Dr. Fantus had opened a blood bank in Chicago. Dr. Fantus had tried to preserve blood on ice. But the red blood cells still broke down rapidly, releasing the deadly potassium. This made the blood unusable after about twenty-four hours.

One of the first things that Dr. Scudder and his new research assistant talked about was a blood bank— where a person could get the right type of blood immediately. The recipient would repay the blood he used by getting friends or relatives to donate blood to the bank. Thus, blood would always be available for others.

Prolonged preservation was the key.

FROM LABORATORY TO BLOOD BANK

It was the breakdown of red blood cells that spoiled refrigerated blood stored in bottles. Also, if blood is not handled gently, the red blood cells tend to break down more easily. Dr. Drew and his staff worked many days and nights studying and experimenting with blood. Blood a day old, seven days old, and several weeks old was tested on animals.

The refrigeration of carefully handled blood at certain temperatures seemed to retard the red cell breakdown. Special containers were designed to keep red cells separated from liquid blood plasma while under refrigeration. After hundreds of animal tests it appeared that blood two weeks old was safe for transfusions.

Experiments on animals, however, could tell just so much. How would two-week old blood react in the human body? What would happen to patients who received two-week old blood? Was it safe? Dr. Drew decided these questions would shape his next experiment.

Presbyterian Hospital had been considering a blood bank for some time. Dr. Drew approached Dr. Scudder with a bold plan for an experimental one. Dr. Scudder submitted Dr. Drew's blood bank idea to the Medical Board of the hospital, and the Board appointed a committee of doctors to study it. Meanwhile Dr. Drew continued his research day and night. Each experiment gave him more and more facts about blood, red cell breakdown, and plasma.

Finally the big day came. The committee of doctors decided to give an experimental blood bank a four-month trial. The bank was set up in the hospital splint room, with Dr. Drew as its Medical Director.

What was the safest way to preserve blood for transfusions? What type of container was best for storing blood? What was the best way to prevent blood from clotting? These were the questions that needed answers.

The first pints of donated blood came from Dr. Drew himself and from members of his blood bank staff. All of the four types, A, B, AB, and O were on the blood bank shelves. In severe emergencies, doctors throughout the hospital called for blood for transfusions. Before and after each transfusion blood samples from the patient were studied thoroughly.

This close watch over patients who had received blood from Dr. Drew's bank brought on an important discovery. Blood over a week old seemed to cause some complications to the patient after the transfusion. It seemed that red blood cells in blood over a week old broke down faster than red blood cells in the patient's own blood, a fact that earlier laboratory tests could not have shown. So Dr. Drew had his laboratory technicians throw away seven day old blood not used in transfusions.

The blood bank very rapidly proved itself to be an immense success. Dr. Drew's method of preserving blood by careful storage and refrigeration had proved to be safe. He was, however, not satisfied. For one thing, to throw out the seven-day old blood was a terrible waste. And in addition, there were bad reactions in some of the patients who had received blood.

AN IMPORTANT OBSERVATION—PLASMA

One day Dr. Drew was observing a container of seven-day old blood about to be thrown away. A layered substance rested on the bottom of the container. Dark red in color, it contained red blood cells and white blood cells. A yellowish liquid filled the rest of the container above the layered cells. This straw-colored liquid was blood plasma. If you can get an old tube of unclotted blood from a hospital laboratory you can observe the same thing for yourself.

Plasma contains everything that whole blood does except the cells, thought Dr. Drew. And, it was the red blood cells that were causing all the trouble.

Dr. Drew then asked himself another very important question. Could plasma alone be used safely in transfusions and with the same results as whole blood? Only careful experimentation would give the answer.

Seven-day old blood was no longer thrown away. It became a source of plasma. Working with Dr. Scudder and other doctors, Dr. Drew spent many weeks examining plasma in every detail.

While the blood bank was busy typing and refrigerating whole blood, the four-month trial period was coming to an end. Four hundred transfusions had been given.

Plasma did not have to be typed since it lacked red cells which contained the substances that determined the blood types A, B, AB, and O. It was easy to collect. Furthermore it was found that dried plasma could be stored more easily and for longer than liquid plasma. And it didn't have to be refrigerated.

PLASMA GOES TO THE BATTLEFIELD

Plasma transfusions had to be tried. Drew talked over his plans for transfusions with Dr. Scudder. They moved ahead. In cases where patients didn't need red blood cell replacement, plasma was used. It worked. Patients in shock, or with wounds or severe burns benefited from plasma alone. Dr. Drew had pioneered a big break-through in medical science. The work of his experimental blood bank was allowed to continue beyond the four-month tryout period.

In January, 1940, Dr. Drew presented his two years of blood research in a thesis called "Banked Blood." Columbia University awarded him a Doctor of Science degree for his blood research. In his thesis he discussed the evolution of the blood bank, changes in preserved blood, his own experimental studies in blood preservation, and the organization, operation, and success of the blood bank at Presbyterian Hospital. His report was used as a guide in setting up new blood banks in the United States and Europe. In 1940 the Presbyterian Blood Bank provided for some 1,800 transfusions. Dr. Drew had gained national and international fame.

The technique of preparing dried plasma still needed to be perfected. Dr. Drew continued experimentation for the Blood Transfusion Association in the use of blood plasma as a substitute for whole blood. In June, 1940, his fellowship was over. He returned to Howard University to continue his teaching career in surgery.

In 1940, World War II was raging in Europe. German planes were attacking and bombing England. Wounded soldiers in hospitals and in the battlefield needed blood badly. The Blood Transfusion Association in New York City offered help. Dr. Drew's old friend from McGill, Dr. John Beattie, was chief of the Royal Air Force Transfusion Service in England. A cablegram from Dr. Beattie to Dr. Drew at Howard read as follows—

> Could you secure five thousand ampoules dried plasma for transfusion work immediately and follow this by equal quantity in three to four weeks. Contents each ampoule should represent about one pint whole plasma.

Dr. Drew's return to teaching was interrupted. His research efforts were about to go into action.

The Blood Transfusion Association in New York asked Dr. Drew to come back to New York to help. He did, and in the fall of 1940 he became medical supervisor of the Blood for Britain Program, to supply blood for the British Red Cross. Under Dr. Drew's guidance dried plasma for airplane shipment to Europe was prepared. In October, 5,000 units of dried plasma was flown across the Atlantic to England. Between October, 1940, and February, 1941, some 1,000 pints of blood were donated by Americans for the war casualties in Europe. The blood collection and plasma processing techniques worked out by Dr. Drew and his staff were in full use. The jump had been made from pure research to practical use.

Once England had set up its own blood banks, a larger blood program for the U.S. Military Forces was planned. The American Red Cross was to carry out this program at Presbyterian Hospital. Dr. Drew became the director of the first American Red Cross Plasma Bank.

In the spring of 1941 a National Blood Bank Program was being planned for U.S. military men throughout the world. The Blood Transfusion Association and the Red Cross were jointly to carry out this program. Naturally, Dr. Drew was named the Medical Director of this effort. He was now ready to put his plasma preservation techniques into even wider use.

THE LAST HURDLE

Charles Drew had cleared many hurdles during the first 39 years of his life. The first were at track meets; then came medical school; and finally the biggest one of all— developing a method of preserving and storing blood plasma for immediate and safe transfusions.

But there was still another hurdle to be faced and cleared. It was one he should not have had to face.

The Armed Forces set up a system of refusing blood donations from non-whites to be used by whites. Blood taken from blacks by the Red Cross was to be collected and stored separately, and given only to blacks. Even Dr. Drew's own blood was to be segregated from the blood of white donors.

This was something that Dr. Drew and his colleagues couldn't fight and win. As a scientist and as director of the Red Cross Bank Program, Dr. Drew gave this statement at a news conference:

> I have been asked my opinion of the practice of separating the blood of Caucasian and Negro donors. My opinion is not important. The fact is that test by race does not stand up in the laboratory.

Dr. Drew had taken a strong stand on the racial separation of blood. He was asked to resign his position as director of the Red Cross Blood Bank Program. He did so quietly. The top expert in the country on blood preservation and blood banks returned once again to teaching surgery at Howard University.

When Japan bombed Pearl Harbor in Hawaii on December 7, 1941, plasma was ready. Hundreds of wounded Americans received the life-saving work of a plasma transfusion. On December 7, 1941, Dr. Charles Drew was still contributing to the welfare of his country. He was busy training young black doctors of the future.

HIS LAST YEARS

Dr. Drew spent the last years of his life speaking and working for the equal treatment of black Americans in all phases of medicine. The practice of segregating blood continued after 1941. Eventually, however, science won over this form of racial prejudice. And today, plasma for transfusions is prepared by pooling the plasma from the bloods of people of all races.

Dr. Drew predicted that someday whole blood and plasma transfusions would be a thing of the past. He even dreamed that someday scientists would create substitutes for the substances making up plasma. The blood bank of his day, he thought, would someday disappear. Dr. Drew had a deep vision and dreamed.

On April 1, 1950, Dr. Drew was driving to an annual medical conference at Tuskegee Institute in Alabama. The car he was driving ran off the road and overturned. In the attempts to save his life, Dr. Drew was given plasma. But his injuries were too severe. He died several hours after the accident at the age of forty-five.

If Dr. Drew had lived to the present he probably would have contributed to the ideas he dreamed about. Since his untimely death much progress has been made in blood science and methods of blood transfusions.

Today the use of whole blood is becoming obsolete. Some medical scientists believe it is safer and more successful to give a patient only the specific blood fraction needed. For example, a patient whose body cannot generate white blood cells—the germ fighters—can receive a transfusion of white cells alone. Likewise, red blood cells could be given alone to a person suffering from anemia. Gamma globulin, a protein substance found in plasma, can be given independently of plasma. This selectivity will reduce the number of transfusions needed and the blood banks as we now know them.

These procedures are laborious and expensive—but certainly offer possibilities for the future. Some scientists are even experimenting with freezing some of a person's blood for a lifetime. Then each person could store some of his own blood for an emergency.

Dr. Charles Drew started something and others who came after him have built on what he left. Although Dr. Drew spent only two years of his life in blood research, his work with blood is part of our medical history.

DR. DANIEL HALE WILLIAMS

1856–1931

He Performed the First Human Heart Operation

On December 3, 1967, in a hospital in Cape Town, South Africa, Dr. Christian Barnard removed a heart from the body of a dead woman, killed when hit by a car. He carried the heart to an adjoining room to a man whose chest had already been opened. Most of his badly diseased heart had already been removed and a heart-lung machine was pumping blood through his body.

Dr. Barnard proceeded to stitch the dead woman's heart onto the auricles of the man—first the left, then the right. He joined the stub of the aorta of this transplanted heart to the aorta of the man. Arteries were connected and then the veins. Four hours passed since Dr. Barnard began his heart transplant operation.

Electrodes were attached to each side of the transplanted heart. An electric current was passed to the heart tissue. The heart muscle jumped and the heart began to beat. About an hour later the man's chest was closed.

Dr. Barnard's boldness and his successes stimulated other heart specialists to try the operation. Undoubtedly you have heard and read about the many heart transplants carried out at medical centers throughout the world. This is all very recent history. But if we go back to 1893, we find another monumental achievement in medical science dealing with the heart. In that year, the first successful open-heart operation on a human was performed. The operation made an already successful black American doctor famous.

Dr. Daniel Hale Williams was at his hospital in Chicago's black community when a man stabbed in the chest with a knife was brought in. The victim's blood pressure began to drop. The pain and coughing of the patient seemed abnormal to Dr. Williams. Perhaps the knife had hit a major blood vessel or even the heart itself, thought Dr. Williams. The victim's condition worsened overnight; he was bleeding internally. Dr. Williams faced an emergency, and he decided to operate.

He opened up the man's chest and repaired his heart. He had done what was seemingly impossible and unthinkable by most surgical authorities of the time. He was the first surgeon to try an open-heart operation which saved a human life—a first in medical history. A Chicago newspaper heralded Dr. Williams' pioneering operation with the headline: "Sewed Up His Heart." His patient lived for more than twenty years afterward.

Before Dr. Williams performed his famous operation, patients with knife wounds in the chest region were kept cool. They were treated with rest, tranquilizers, and prayers. Usually they died.

Dr. Williams had been bold, and skillful in what he had done. He had studied the human body, especially its anatomy, long and hard before his historic operation. His daring and immediate success changed both professional and public attitudes about heart surgery.

FROM BARBER TO SURGEON

It had been only ten years before his famous operation that Daniel Hale Williams had received his degree in medicine from Chicago Medical College. After graduation he was appointed as an instructor in human anatomy at the same school. Perhaps this was a clue to his exceptional ability in medical studies.

For Dan Williams, life as a medical student had been a financial hardship. But he had lived through much hardship since the age of twelve, when his father died. His earlier years, in contrast, had been happy, secure, and normal.

Dan Williams was born in 1856 as a free black child since his parents were free people living in Pennsylvania at his birth. As a young child he was able to attend school regularly, which was not the case for most black children at that time in America.

His father had become a prosperous barber. He was also a strong and active leader and speaker on equal rights and opportunities for black people in this country. In 1867, when his father died, his mother was unable to provide for her seven children. Some were sent to live with relatives, and others to a convent school. Eleven-year-old Dan was left with a shoemaker friend of his mother's in Baltimore to learn the shoemaking trade. At this point, his schooling ended for a while.

The years that followed were unsettling for Dan Williams. He had no family and no schooling to hold him in one place for long. He moved from job to job and even did some barbering like his father. As a teenager he constantly recalled something his father had often said: "We colored people must cultivate the mind." These words always stuck with Dan Williams and motivated him to get an education.

At seventeen, he was tired of wandering and went to live with an older sister in Wisconsin. Later they moved to Janesville, Wisconsin, and it was here that Dan Williams met a well-known black barber named Charles Anderson. And in becoming a barber under Mr. Anderson, he found out what he could do with his hands. Handling scissors, comb, and razor helped him to develop fine hand coordination. Cutting hair and shaving men's faces required agile and gentle finger movements. These were also requirements for a skillful surgeon.

Working in Anderson's barbershop was a kind of school for Dan Williams. He learned much from listening to his customers' conversations. He borrowed their books and read whenever there was no hair to cut. College was ever on his mind, and Mr. Anderson allowed him to work part-time so that he could attend high school. Dan arranged for special tutoring, and with this extra help, he was able to graduate from a classical academy in 1877.

Coming frequently to Anderson's barbershop for his haircut was a Dr. Palmer. Barber Williams had heard about Dr. Palmer trying to save a life of a man with a gun shot wound. The case excited him, and he discussed it one day with Dr. Palmer as he cut his hair. Dr. Palmer's work inspired Dan Williams. He decided he wanted to become a doctor.

Dr. Palmer agreed to take Dan Williams on as an apprentice doctor in his office. In those days working in a doctor's office was the first step in medical training. It is interesting to note that in the history of medicine the first surgeons were barbers. Early barbers often performed minor operations. The red and white striped poles which you see today outside barber shops are symbols of the early barber's operations.

Dan Williams worked and studied hard under Dr. Palmer. Dr. Palmer worked quickly and was a decisive man. Surgery was a crude and often brutal business in the 1800's. These were the days before antiseptics. Infection was difficult to fight, so opening up the body to remove a diseased organ or bullet was never tried.

After two years, Dr. Palmer felt that his young assistants were ready for medical school. His two white apprentices were going to Chicago Medical College. Dan Williams wanted to go with them, but money was a problem. Medical school was as expensive to attend then as it is today. However, by working at odd jobs and borrowing some money from Mr. Anderson, Dan was able to leave Janesville and enter the Chicago Medical College.

He often wrote the Andersons to inform them of his progress; they were like foster parents to him. His letters often had to contain requests for money for rent, food, books, tuition, and laboratory fees. His financial plight made it hard for him to concentrate on his studies in anatomy, physiology, histology, materia medica, and chemistry. Anatomy was his favorite subject.

The second year of medical school was a bit easier. Summer work had allowed him to earn and save some money, and he had regained his health from a bout of sickness during the past spring. Clinical training in hospitals began during this middle year. Bedside instruction and watching operations being performed were especially exciting to him. He learned about infections and methods of disinfection. Modern surgical techniques were just beginning to be taught in medical schools.

In March, 1883, thirty-six men marched down the aisle of the Chicago Grand Opera House to take the Hippocratic Oath. Dr. Daniel H. Williams was one of the thirty-six proud men to receive a medical degree from Chicago Medical College.

OPERATING ON THE DINING ROOM TABLE

The new Dr. Williams decided to stay in Chicago to practice medicine. Black Americans were migrating by the thousands to Chicago and other northern cities from the South, and Dr. Williams felt he would be needed to serve his people. There were only a handful of black doctors in Chicago in 1883. Dr. Williams opened his office on Chicago's South Side, an integrated neighborhood.

Since black doctors were not appointed to any hospital staffs, they were unable to work in the white-owned and white-run hospitals. Furthermore, it was difficult for their black patients to gain admission to the few hospitals that were established in Chicago at the time. So when Dr. Williams' patients required surgery, he would perform his operations in the kitchen or dining room of a patient's home or apartment. Surgery was still pretty much a trial and error business for all doctors. Dr. Williams' operations were quite successful, and his reputation spread rapidly across the city. He started to attract the attention of the entire medical profession in the Chicago area and throughout the state of Illinois.

Then Dr. Williams' professional growth became in danger of being stunted. He had little access to further medical learning and the newer surgical techniques that were being developed and made available to those doctors who were members of white medical groups working in white hospitals. This presented a dilemma for him, since he naturally wanted to improve his ability and skills as a doctor and surgeon.

In time, Dr. Williams managed to gain an appointment to the surgical staff of the South Side Dispensary.

This gave him the opportunity to perform more operations under somewhat better conditions than in a patient's home. He continued to give instruction in anatomy at Chicago Medical College, as he had done since graduation. In 1889, he was appointed to the Illinois State Board of Health. He served on the Board for four years and was a leader in improving medical care and health standards for the people of Illinois.

By 1890 several things were distressing Dr. Williams. Young black women who wanted to become nurses could not gain admission to any nursing school in Chicago. Secondly, more young black doctors were graduating each year from medical school, but no black doctor could practice in an all-white hospital at that time. Moreover, these new doctors needed nurses. Hospitals were and still are training grounds for doctors and nurses. Thirdly, Dr. Williams had a woman patient who needed an operation that couldn't be done in her dining room or kitchen. The woman needed the services that a hospital could provide, but none were open to her. As long as Dr. Williams was not accepted on a hospital staff, these problems would remain.

Dr. Williams was committed to progress for black people in every phase of medicine—public health, daily medical services, training nurses, training doctors, and providing the best possible surgery. The solution to his dilemma was a simple one: he would open his own hospital.

The hospital that Dr. Williams dreamed of was to be different from any hospital in America at the time. It was to serve the needs of both white and black people. The conditions for black patients, black doctors, and black nurses were foremost in his mind. However, he felt that his hospital should be for all people regardless of their color. His hospital would train and employ white nurses as well as black ones, and white doctors as well as black ones. He wanted a hospital for black people, but he did not want a black hospital. There would be no more operations done in a dining room or kitchen.

PROVIDENT HOSPITAL

Once Dr. Williams had made up his mind to open his own interracial hospital, he moved quickly into action. He went to his friends, black and white, who were businessmen, ministers, lawyers, doctors, civic leaders, and teachers at Chicago Medical College. Working committees were set up. There were endless details in handling committee work and fund-raising events. Donations came from both black and white people. Creating a hospital was a heavy burden for Dr. Williams, for he still had his sick patients to care for each day.

A three-story building that would have twelve beds to start with was finally chosen. The floors and walls were scrubbed and painted by volunteers. People donated furniture, sheets, pillows, food, soap, and other necessities. Dr. Williams purchased medical supplies and surgical tools with some of the money raised for the hospital. In May, 1891, the Provident Hospital and Training School Association opened its doors.

Dr. Williams staffed his hospital with only the most competent doctors. The training program for nurses was rigorous and lasted for eighteen months. His standards were always high.

Today Provident Hospital and Training School has more than 200 beds and admits close to 6,000 patients each year. It is now a complete facility with a pathology laboratory, pharmacy, physical therapy department, emergency room, post-operative recovery room, a social work department, and a hospital auxiliary.

Most of the cases at Provident Hospital during the first two years were surgical. Dr. Williams' interest in surgery became intense. He was a keen observer, noting every detail, and making no diagnosis until he had all of the facts. His ability to diagnose a patient's illness was outstanding.

At Provident Hospital, Dr. Williams established his remarkable reputation as a surgeon. Doctors from all over the state crowded into his small operating room to watch him perform an operation. His hand motions were quick and smooth—beautiful to watch. Before making an incision, Dr. Williams always informed himself of the patient's full medical history. He was ingenious and daring, but never reckless. Because of his thorough knowledge of human anatomy he knew what to expect when he cut into tissues and organs.

It was at Provident Hospital that Dr. Daniel Hale Williams performed his famous and pioneering heart operation.

AN EMERGENCY HEART OPERATION

Dr. Williams leaned over the chest of a man rushed to Provident Hospital during the evening of July 9, 1893. The victim, James Cornish, had been stabbed near the heart during a fight near Provident Hospital. Dr.

Williams' eyes were steadily fixed on the knife wound in the man's chest. At first the wound, just to the left of the breastbone, did not look serious. The knife had left a cut about an inch long.

At the hospital the wound had nearly stopped bleeding. There was no sign of internal bleeding, but Dr. Williams could not be sure of this. The X-ray technique was not available to doctors in 1893.

The wound appeared to be superficial. The patient was unable to tell what kind of knife had stabbed him. Neither did he know how long the blade was. With rest the wound should heal, thought Dr. Williams.

But during the night, Cornish's condition took a turn for the worse. Bleeding started again and continued off and on. Severe pains over the heart area developed. His pulse weakened. Signs of shock appeared. The patient was near collapse. Perhaps the stabbing was deeper than Dr. Williams could see with his probe.

When a person goes into shock, his blood pressure is at a low point. This is dangerous, for the body's circulatory system is losing blood. When this happens, death is a real possibility. This is what Dr. Williams was facing as he re-examined his patient in the early morning hours.

Dr. Williams concluded that something was wrong in the region of the man's heart. But what? Perhaps the knife had punctured or cut a major blood vessel. Perhaps it had struck the heart tissue itself.

Cornish's condition grew steadily weaker. There was now evidence of internal bleeding. His pulse could scarcely be felt in his wrist. Pains over the heart and short, sharp coughs persisted. He was exhausted from a sleepless night.

On the morning following the patient's admission to Provident Hospital, Dr. Williams decided to operate. He would open up the left side of the dying man's chest cavity to explore the heart area.

Quickly he called his staff of doctors and nurses into his small operating room. Six of Dr. Williams' friends were alerted. They crowded into the operating room to watch. The operation was begun immediately with the nurses standing by to hand and receive surgical tools from Dr. Williams. He worked virtually unaided since there were no blood transfusions to be given, no trained anesthetist, no X-rays to be taken, no drugs to be given. And there was no heart-lung machine to maintain blood circulation during the operation as is available to today's heart surgeon. Nor was there an electrocardiograph machine to measure electrical impulses from the heart. This is one way today's surgeon can tell how the patient is doing during the operation.

Dr. Williams pressed the scalpel point to the bare chest of his limp patient. The first cut was made between two ribs. He lengthened the original wound, making the one-inch stab wound about six inches long. A second incision was made. This exposed part of the breastbone, a portion of a rib near the bone, and some cartilage between the ribs. A small patch of cartilage between the rib and bone was cut, opening a small hole into the chest cavity. The opening was about two inches long and one and one-half inches wide. The cartilage was difficult to work with since it was elastic in nature and closed up quickly when cut.

Through the opening made in the cartilage, Dr. Williams could see some large major blood vessels. He worked rapidly, tying off and moving blood vessels to make room to get to the heart itself. One of the blood vessels had been pierced by the knife and had been leaking blood. Dr. Williams tied the injured vessel with catgut to stop the bleeding.

The pericardium, a thin, protective, membranous sac which envelops the heart was in sight. The sac, too, had received a stroke of the knife blade. The sac wound was about one and a quarter inches long. Since the sac tissue lies directly next to the heart, the heart, too, had been hit by the point of the knife blade. The punctured wound in the heart was about one-tenth of an inch long. The heart itself, however, was not bleeding and needed no stitches.

But the protective sac around the heart was another matter. The cut in the pericardium would have to be sewed up. Dr. Williams flooded the exposed heart area with salt solution to guard against infection. Then gently grasping the pericardial tissue with surgical forceps, he closed the cut with catgut. He was then ready to close up the chest opening he had made. Using silkworm gut, the cartilage and skin incisions made to reach the heart were sutured. A dry dressing was placed over the outside incision.

By the seventh day after the operation Cornish's pulse rate was nearly normal. His fever was down and his body temperature was back to normal. His heart beat sounds were strong and regular. About three weeks later, Dr. Williams performed a minor operation to remove fluid that had collected in Cornish's chest cavity. Eighty ounces of bloody fluid were removed.

Fifty-one days after he was stabbed, James Cornish was released from Provident Hospital. Two years later,

Dr. Williams saw his heart patient working hard in a stockyard, and for twenty years after, James Cornish lived a normal life.

Dr. Daniel H. Williams was the first man to operate successfully on the human heart.

DR. WILLIAMS' PLACE IN SURGERY

In 1893, no surgeon would have dared to think of sewing up a wound of the heart's pericardium. With the most modern methods of examination available in 1893, it was extremely difficult to diagnose wounds of the pericardium and heart. Touching the heart was "out of bounds." Dr. Williams was risking his reputation and his career if his patient had died on the operating table. An operation such as his ran an enormous risk of death from infection.

The historical literature of medicine does not contain a single successful attempt at human heart surgery before 1893. Dr. Williams, however, did not report his work on Cornish until three and one-half years after the operation. An illness about the time of Cornish's recovery and a new position as chief surgeon at Freedman's Hospital in Washington, D.C., prevented him from writing and getting his report published earlier. So in March, 1897, the *Medical Record*, which was a weekly journal of medicine and surgery, contained an article entitled, "Stab Wound of the Heart and Pericardium—Suture of the Pericardium—Recovery—Patient Alive Three Years Afterward," by Dr. Daniel H. Williams.

In September, 1896, a German surgeon, Dr. Louis Rehn, performed an operation similar to that of Dr. Williams. Dr. Rehn's patient had also received a knife-stab wound in the heart. The wound in this patient's heart was larger than the one in Cornish's. Dr. Rehn successfully sutured the heart tissue itself.

News of Dr. Rehn's operation spread throughout Germany, Europe, and America. In 1895 and 1896 there were reports from other surgeons who had tried sutures in and around the heart and had failed.

Dr. Williams did not take part in the clamor for recognition as did Dr. Rehn and other doctors who had been unsuccessful. He had no time for foolish disputes about who was first. All that Dr. Williams cared about was that he had saved a human life by his heart operation.

The operations of Drs. Rehn and Williams might well have turned into an international dispute about who was first if Dr. Williams had been a white man.

In 1908, Dr. Williams celebrated his twenty-fifth year in medicine. Doctors from all parts of the United States gathered in Chicago to honor him at a testimonial dinner. Several years later he was appointed to the surgical staff at the white St. Luke's hospital in Chicago. In 1913, he was made a member of the American College of Surgeons.

During the years after his monumental operation, Dr. Williams continued to contribute to the development and improvement of surgery and medical practice in our country. He spoke at medical conventions, wrote articles for medical journals, and helped to train many new surgeons. At one time he had patients—black and white—in five different hospitals at once.

In 1920, Dr. Williams retired to his favorite summer vacation spot on a lake in Idlewild, Michigan—a summer resort town in the northern woods of that state. Here he built a small cottage on a hill overlooking the lake. His well earned days of rest were spent fishing and caring for his flower garden. Here too, he became a doctor to anyone in need of medical help. He opened a little hospital for emergencies and placed a fire bell in a high tower so he could be called when a sick or injured vacationer needed attention.

In 1924, Dr. Williams' wife died and two years later he suffered a severe stroke. The next five years were sad ones for him. Other strokes followed. The pain and misery that he had prevented so many people from having were with him during his last years. His was a slow death that could not be helped by medical science. Finally on August 4, 1931, Dr. Williams died in Idlewild, the place he loved so much.

News wires flashed the death of this great pioneer surgeon. Newspapers recounted his medical work and service to everyone of all races.

Part of a tribute printed in the *Lake County Star*, the paper that served the Idlewild community, read as follows—

> . . . an invalid for nearly five years . . . His departure from Idlewild was attended with honors and reverence of exceptional character . . . .
>
> It is remarkable that so famous a man should carry his honors so lightly. In 1920 he built his beautiful cottage in Idlewild . . . He did not practice, but he never turned a deaf ear to a call for help. One of our bankers owes his life to the ministrations of "Dr. Dan," and many others found him willing and ready to serve without pay in the cause of humanity. Modest, retiring, unassuming, he found his little world here full of reverent, loving friends. To the children he was "Dr.

Dan," and a friend even though regarded awesomely as a miracle man.

Like many other truly great men he found peace, solace, and instruction in nature. He loved his flowers and his garden was filled with lovely plants. He loved the woods and waters and the living things in them . . . .

To have known him was a pleasure—to know him intimately was a priceless privilege. He was at once an inspiration and an aid. To emulate his simplicity, his kindly spirit and his great modesty is to pay tribute to the truly great. The world has lost greatly.

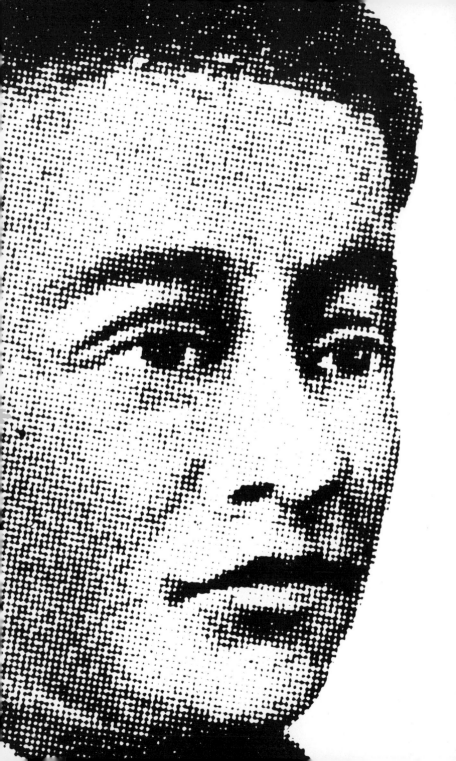

BENJAMIN BANNEKER

1731–1806

He Studied the Heavens

His neighbors called him a lazy old man. When they peeped into his cabin during the day, they saw him sound asleep. They talked about his peculiar living habits and how he had changed. During his younger days he was known to put in a full day's work every day on his farm near Baltimore, Maryland. But now he no longer tended cows or tilled the soil the way he used to. Good farmers, they thought, should be up early and working and in bed soon after dark.

But little did his neighbors know that at night while they slept Benjamin Banneker was awake and outdoors. It was not laziness but astronomy that accounted for his daytime sleep. Each night as darkness approached, Banneker would leave his cabin. Wrapped in a cloak, he would lie flat on his back most of the night gazing at heavenly bodies with his telescope. He was studying the motions of the moon, sun, stars, and planets. At sunrise he returned to his cabin and went to bed. Throughout the morning hours while everyone else was hard at work, Benjamin Banneker was sound asleep. Occasionally during the afternoon hours he would hoe his small garden and trim his fruit trees.

During the day when he wasn't sleeping, Banneker was shut up in his cabin. Alone, he would study astronomy books and make calculations. He was so immersed in his studies that neighborhood boys could trespass on his land and strip his trees of their fruit without his even noticing. Even the cold winter nights did not stop Benjamin Banneker from making his astronomical observations. From a window he made in the roof of his cabin, he could still observe the night sky during the winter. Banneker did not worry about his neighbors gossiping about his daily routine. He was too busy making his nightly observations and calculations.

During the late 1700's, few white men studied science books. Very few considered science, much less astronomy, as an occupation. For a black man to be studying the sun, moon, stars, and planets—this was very unusual!

In 1791, James McHenry, a prominent Maryland politician, sent a letter to Goddard and Angell, operators of a publishing company in Baltimore. The letter read something like this:

Baltimore, August 20, 1791

Messrs. Goddard and Angell,

BENJAMIN BANNEKER, a free Negro, has calculated an Almanac, for the coming year, 1792. He desires to put it to good use and has requested me to aid his application to you to have it published. I have satisfied myself with respect to his title to this kind of authorship. If you can agree with him on a price for his work, I assure you it will do you credit. At the same time you will be encouraging Banneker's talents that have thus far surmounted the most discouraging circumstances and prejudice.

This man is about fifty-nine years of age. He was born in Baltimore County. His father was an African, and his mother the offspring of African parents. His father and mother, having obtained their freedom, were able to send him to an obscure school, where he learned, as a boy, reading, writing, and arithmetic. At their death, his parents left him a few acres of farm land. From his farming he has supported himself ever since by means of constant labor and producing fine crops.

What he had learned at school, he did not forget. During hours of leisure which occurred during his most toilsome farm life, he worked at mathematical problems, applying the principles of the few rules of arithmetic he had been taught at school. This kind of mental exercise formed his chief amusement. His facility with arithmetical calculations made him often serviceable to his neighbors. He attracted the attention of the Ellicott family, known for their remarkable ingenuity and knowledge in mechanics. It is about three years since Mr. George Ellicott lent Banneker some of his books and tables on astronomy and some astronomical instruments. From thenceforth, he employed his leisure in astronomical researches.

He now took up the idea of the calculations for an Almanac, and actually completed an entire set for the last year, upon his original stock of arithmetic. Encouraged by his first attempt, he entered upon his calculation for 1792. His latest Almanac, as well as the former, he began and finished without the least information, or assistance, from any person, or other books than those from Mr. Ellicott. So whatever merit is attached to his present performance, is exclusively and peculiarly his own. . . .

I consider this Negro as a fresh proof that the powers of the mind are disconnected with the color of the skin. . . . In every civilized country we shall find thousands of whites, liberally educated, and who have enjoyed greater opportunities of instruction than this Negro. Yet many are inferior to him in those intellectual acquirements and capacities that form the most characteristic feature in the human race. But the system that would assign to these degraded blacks an origin different from the whites, must be relinquished as similar circumstances multiply. Banneker is a striking contradiction to the doctrine, that 'the Negroes are naturally inferior to whites, and unsusceptible to accomplishments in arts and sciences.' If nothing is to impede the progress of humanity, then bettering the condition of slavery will necessarily lead to its extinction.— Let, however, the issue be what it may, I cannot but wish, on this occasion, to see the Public patronage keep pace with my black friend's merit.

I am, Gentlemen, your most obedient servant,

James McHenry

Benjamin Bannaker's
PENNSYLVANIA, DELAWARE, MARY-
LAND, AND VIRGINIA
ALMANAC,
FOR THE
YEAR of our LORD 1795;
Being the Third after Leap-Year.

BANNAKER.

PHILADELPHIA:

Printed for WILLIAM GIBBONS, Cherry Street

Iſt Month, JANUARY, hath 31 Days.

	d.	h.	m.	
Laſt Q.	3	1	18	Morn
New ☽	10	1	15	Morn
Firſt Q.	17	11	2	Morn.
Full ○	24	5	19	Morn.

☊ { 1 . 21 ; 11 ♋ 20 ; 21 19 } Deg.

PLANETS PLACES

D.	☉	♄	♃	♂	♀	☿	☽'s
	♑	♊	♒	♏	♒	♑	La.
1	11	8	11	5	0	2	5 N
7	17	7	12	9	9	12	3 N
13	23	7	14	12	16	22	4 S
19	29	7	15	15	22	♒ 2	4 S.
25	♒ 6	7	16	19	♓ 0	12	3 N.

M D	W D	*Remarkable days, Aſpects, Wea. &c.*	☉ riſes	☉ ſets	☽'s place	☽ riſe	☽ ſouth	☽'s age.
1	6	Circumciſion	7 20	4 40	♎ 7	riſe	morn	22
2	7	*windy*	7 20	4 40	19	morn	6 19	23
3	C	1ſt Sund p Chriſt	7 20	4 40	♏ 1	1 25	7 1	24
4	2	*and*	7 19	4 41	13	2 25	7 44	25
5	3	*cold*	7 19	4 41	25	3 23	8 28	26
6	4	Epiphany	7 18	4 42	♐ 7	4 19	9 12	27
7	5	□ ♂ ♀ *rain*	7 18	4 42	18	5 13	9 58	28
8	6	Arcturus ri. 11 18	7 17	4 43	♑ 0	6 6	10 4	29
9	7	*or*	7 17	4 43	12	6 57	11 32	30
10	C	1ſt Sund p. E. ☉	7 16	4 44	24	ſets	af 22	☽
11	2	☌ ☽ ♃	7 15	4 45	♒ 7	6 7	1 12	2
12	3	*ſnow*	7 15	4 45	20	7 11	2 2	3
13	4	☌ ☉ ☿ Occident.	7 14	4 46	♓ 3	8 15	2 50	4
14	5	*flying*	7 13	4 47	16	9 20	3 39	5
15	6	Day incr 18 min.	7 13	4 47	♈ 0	10 27	4 28	6
16	7	*clouds*	7 12	4 48	14	11 36	5 18	7
17	C	2d Sund p Epip.	7 11	4 49	28	mor	6 10	8
18	2	*followed*	7 10	4 50	♉ 12	0 47	7 3	9
19	3	□ ♃ ♂ *by*	7 10	4 50	27	1 57	7 57	10
20	4	☉ enter ♒ *ſnow*	7 9	4 51	♊ 11	3 6	8 52	11
21	5	Pleiades ſou. 7 20	7 8	4 52	25	4 11	9 50	12
22	6	*or*	7 7	4 53	♋ 10	5 14	10 50	13
23	7	Days 9 48 *cold*	7 6	4 54	25	6 13	11 50	14
24	C	Septuag. Sund.	7 5	4 55	♌ 9	riſe	morn	15
25	2	*rain,*	7 4	4 56	23	6 54	0 48	16
26	3	Sirius ſou. 10 h.	7 3	4 57	♍ 7	8 1	1 42	17
27	4		7 2	4 58	20	9 6	2 22	18
28	5	*ſnow*	7 1	4 59	♎ 3	10 9	3 19	19
29	6	Day 10 h *toward*	7 0	5 0	16	11 9	4 4	20
30	7	*the*	6 59	5 1	28	morn	4 48	21
31	C	Sexag. Sund. *end*	6 58	5 2	♏ 10	0 7	5 30	22

Banneker's almanac for the month
of January shows phases of the moon,
positions of planets, a calendar of days,
and predicts weather conditions.

And so it was that Benjamin Banneker, at sixty years of age, had his first Almanac published for the year 1792. And each year afterwards until 1802 Banneker's Almanac was published. For a black American in the 1790's this was a remarkable scientific achievement. Banneker's Almanacs were widely read in Pennsylvania, Delaware, Maryland, Virginia, and in other states. In many homes it was found next to the family Bible.

Banneker's Almanacs contained astronomical calculations representing high scientific and mathematical ability. In addition to being a guidebook to the heavenly events of the time, they were a source of weather and tidal information. Weather forecasts were important to farmers and travelers during Banneker's time, just as they are today. Essays on nature and natural phenomena in his almanac were based on his sharp-eyed personal observations. One issue of his almanac discussed the "locust"-plague cycle, calculated by Banneker to be every 17 years. Another Banneker Almanac contained a description of the habits of bees as he observed them on his farm. Witty sayings in prose and verse were also found in his publication.

BANNEKER'S EARLY LIFE

Few of the actual facts and events of Benjamin Banneker's early life are known. What is known for certain was reported in his family's Bible.

Benjamin Banneker was born free of slavery in the thinly populated wilderness country of Maryland, about ten miles from Baltimore. He was raised and lived all of his life on his family's farm on the Patapsco River in Baltimore County. His parents, who were free black people (his father had been a slave who bought his free-dom), purchased the 102 acres of farmland in 1737 with 17,000 pounds of tobacco. On a hill overlooking the Patapsco River, Banjamin's father built the family home. Benjamin was six years old at the time.

The Banneker farm was known to be one of the best in the community, producing vegetables, fruit, poultry, and honey from bee hives. Farming was the sole means by which Banneker's father supported his family of six. Throughout his boyhood, Banneker worked side by side with his parents in the chores of farming. He attended school only during the winter months, when there was little farm work to be done.

In a one-room school nearby, Benjamin Banneker learned how to read, write, and do simple mathematics. He was especially good at solving mathematical pro-blems. His eagerness for books and learning showed up quickly. As a schoolboy, he seldom played with his schoolmates, preferring instead to read whatever books he could get hold of. Few books were available when Banneker was growing up. It was not easy even for whites to get a good education in Maryland at the time. Despite his studious habits, young Benjamin became an industrious and excellent farmer. While he worked hard with his hands in the soil, his brain was hard at work making up and solving problems in mathematics. The farming community in which he lived provided little opportunity for scholars—white or black. But it seems that Banneker was able to overcome the lack of books at home and the little schooling he received by learning things firsthand. He had an intense curiosity and was a close observer of everything in nature—sky, earth, clouds, rain, and the seasons. And he had a reputation in his community for being extremely intelligent, with a quick and sharp mind for working with numbers. News of his mathematical ability spread throughout the county and into surrounding states. Farmers came to him with brain-teasing puzzles and practical problems to solve.

At the age of twenty-two Benjamin Banneker had finished constructing a clock. It was the first of its kind in the Maryland region. Its construction gave him a chance to apply some of his mathematical ability, and demonstrated his genius for mechanics. It is reported that he took apart and studied the pieces of a pocket watch made in England and lent to him by a traveling merchant. He used the watch as a model for his clock. The parts of his clock were made of hard wood cut and shaped with a knife. He had no delicate tools to help him with such an intricate piece of mechanism.

The building of the clock turned out to be of great importance in the life of Benjamin Banneker. By 1772, the clock had been keeping time for about twenty years. Its fame attracted the attention of neighbors throughout Baltimore County. People in Maryland, Delaware, Pennsylvania, and Virginia heard about the clock built by a black man, which struck at the hours of six and twelve. They came from miles around to see it. Banneker enjoyed the company of these visitors since he was unmarried and lived alone on the farm which he had inherited from his parents.

Visitors described Banneker as a "brave-looking pleasant man . . . very noble in appearance. . . . A perfect gentleman . . . kind, generous, hospitable, humane, dignified, and pleasing to talk with."

BANNEKER MEETS AN ASTRONOMER

Amongst those who came to see Banneker's clock were members of the distinguished Ellicott family—George, Andrew, John, and Benjamin. The Ellicotts were a well-educated Quaker family with engineering, scientific, and business talent. They moved from Pennsylvania and settled near Banneker's farm in 1772 to build and operate flour mills along the Patapsco River. They had heard about their new neighbor's clock when they lived in Pennsylvania.

Benjamin Banneker spent many hours watching the construction of the Ellicott's flour mills and the operation of the mill machinery. The Ellicott's flour business grew rapidly. A store and post office were opened at the mill site. Supplies sold at the store and food for the mill workers came from Banneker's farm. Today, Ellicott City stands at the site of the Ellicott flour enterprise near the Patapsco River in Maryland.

Having the Ellicotts as neighbors and getting to talk with them at their store was a turning point in Benjamin Banneker's life. The store and post office became popular meeting places for the community people to discuss the news of the day. George Ellicott was a mathematician and astronomer. He was impressed by the curiosity and scientific interests of his black neighbor, and he respected Banneker's mechanical genius and science-math aptitude. The common interests of Banneker and George Ellicott led them into a strong friendship.

George Ellicott encouraged the interests and talents of his friend Banneker by lending him a number of astronomy books and instruments. Among the books were Mayer's *Tables of the Sun and Moon*, Ferguson's *Astronomy*, and Leadbetter's *Lunar Tables*. These books, which were important and scholarly works of the time, were the first of their kind that Banneker had ever seen. They opened up a new world to him. George Ellicott had intended to instruct Banneker in how to use the rather difficult books, but he never got around to it. But this didn't slow Banneker down for long. Mr. Ellicott was later surprised to find that Banneker had discovered how to use the books without his assistance. Within a few years, Banneker could predict when eclipses of the sun and moon would occur.

The study of astronomy captured Benjamin Banneker and came to dominate his life completely. In studying the books given to him by his friend Ellicott, he claimed to have found errors of calculation. He mentioned these errors in notes to George Ellicott. One of his notes read:

> It appears to me that the wisest men may at times be in error; for instance, Dr. Ferguson informes us that, when the sun is within 12° of either node at the time of full moon, the moon will be eclipsed; but I find that, according to his method of projecting a lunar eclipse, there will be none by the above elements, and yet the sun is within 11° 468′ 11″ of the moon's ascending node. But the moon, being in her apogee, prevents the appearancee of this eclipse.

Later in another note to Ellicott, Banneker wrote:

> Errors that ought to be corrected in my astronomical tables are these: 2d vol. Leadbetter, p. 204, when Saturn anomaly is 4ˢ30° the equation 3° 30′ 4″ ought to have been 3° 28′ 41″. In Mars equation, P. 155, the logarithm of his distance from Sun ought to have been 6 in the second place from the index, instead of 7, that is, from the time that its anomaly is 3ˢ24° until it is 4ˢ0°.

As the years moved on, Benjamin Banneker advanced in his astronomical studies. George Ellicott urged him to undertake the calculations of an almanac. To do so, Banneker would have to give up farming and spend all of his time studying astronomy and mathematics. And this he did at the age of fifty-two by selling his farm to the Ellicotts. They paid him enough money each year thereafter to live on and allowed him to continue living in the cabin he had occupied all of his life. Free of laborious farming chores, Banneker could now study the heavens at night and sleep and do his calculations during the day. For the next twenty years he devoted his full time to the science of astronomy.

Up until 1790, Benjamin Banneker had never traveled outside of his home state of Maryland, much less very far from his farm. His fame was local, but national recognition was in his future.

In July, 1790, the U.S. Congress passed a bill to set up a capital city on the Potomac River. Portions of land from the states of Maryland and Virginia were relinquished by these states to make up the new capital of our country. President George Washington selected a team of engineers and surveyors to lay out the streets of the new capital and to plan the location of the new government buildings. One of the Ellicott brothers, Major Andrew Ellicott was appointed to the survey commission by President Washington. Andrew Ellicott, knowing Banneker's talents, recommended to Thomas Jefferson, then Secretary of State, that Benjamin Banneker be named to assist him in laying out the new Federal Territory (now Washington, D.C.), as it was known then. And so it was that President Washington, at Jefferson's suggestion, appointed Banneker to the Federal commission that would plan and lay out the capital of the United States.

On March 12, 1791, the Georgetown Weekly Ledger announced the arrival of Ellicott and L'Enfant (a famous French engineer who headed the commission), accompanied by "Benjamin Banneker, an Ethiopian whose abilities as surveyor and astronomer already prove that Mr. Jefferson's concluding that that race of men were void of mental endowment was without foundation."

Benjamin Banneker helped in selecting the sites for the U.S. Capitol building, the U.S. Treasury building, the White House, and other Federal buildings. At the time, most black Americans were held as slaves in this country. Banneker showed that free black Americans, with much less formal education than many whites, could make significant contributions to the development, life, and culture of the new nation. When L'Enfant quit his job as head of the commission over a dispute with Federal officials, he took the printed plans with him. Washington was afraid that the commission's work on the new Federal city would come to a standstill. But Benjamin Banneker had memorized the plans that he, Ellicott, and L'Enfant had worked out and was able to finish the job without L'Enfant. During his leisure hours when he was not surveying and laying out the streets of the District of Columbia, Banneker was hard at work with his astronomical investigations.

On his return from the Federal city, Banneker completed his first almanac. With the help of James McHenry he arranged for its publication in 1792.

BANNEKER'S ALMANACS

An almanac is a book or table with a calendar of days and months to which astronomical information is added. It shows the time of the rising and setting of the sun and moon, phases of the moon, positions of planets, eclipses, the time of high and low tides, and other useful bits of information.

The compiling of almanacs started thousands of years ago when astronomy began. The first printed almanac appeared in 1457. A German astronomer and mathematician produced one which was used by Columbus. The first American almanac was printed in Cambridge,

Massachusetts, in 1639. With information from an almanac as a guide, a farmer could reset a stopped clock, tell the time of day, and estimate the proper time of season to plant and harvest his crops.

Benjamin Banneker calculated almanacs for each year beginning in 1792 and ending in 1802. They were printed and sold well throughout that period. In each edition he included tables with the following information:

> The motions of the sun and moon
> The true places and aspects of the planets
> The rising and setting of the sun
> Rising, setting, and southing of the moon
> Lunations, conjunctions, and eclipses
> and
> The rising, setting, and southing of the
> planets and noted fixed stars

On page 50 is a copy of a page from Banneker's Almanac for 1795. Each of his almanacs carried a table of information like this for each month of the year. Get a copy of this year's *Old Farmer's Almanac* from your library. Compare it with the page from Banneker's *Almanac*. Does it contain any information like that included by Banneker?

Besides astronomical calculations there were other items of unusual interest in Banneker's almanacs. One of these was a kind of horoscope as shown on page 61. A horoscope is a diagram or scheme which divides the heavens into twelve parts. Each part was believed to be governed by one of twelve constellations or signs. A constellation is a group of stars. The Greeks identified specific animals or objects with each of the constellations according to the figures they seemed to see in their minds as they looked at the different groups of stars. Here are the names of the constellations with their popular names beside them. Only two of the constellations, Gemini and Scorpio, look anything like the real thing after which they are named:

ARIES—The Ram
TAURUS—The Bull
GEMINI—The Twins
CANCER—The Crab
LEO—The Lion
VIRGO—The Virgin
LIBRA—The Scales
SCORPIO—The Scorpion
SAGITTARIUS—The Archer
CAPRICORN—The Goat
AQUARIUS—The Waterman
PISCES—The Fishes

Count the number of figures or signs drawn around the figure of the human body on page 61. How many are there? This illustration probably reflects the thinking at Banneker's time. Each constellation was supposed to have an effect on the condition of different parts of the human body. Read the instructions given by Banneker under his horoscope illustration. If you had lived in Banneker's time you would have used a table like this one to find the sign or constellation.

Here is the explanation of the horoscope as written by Banneker. As you read each line, refer to the illustration and find the sign he is referring to:

Man's head and face Heaven's ram obey,
His neck the neck-strong bull does sway
The arm twining twins guides hands and arms
Breasts, sides, and stomach Cancer charms

The ANATOMY of MAN's BODY, as governed by the Twelve Constellations.

♈ The Head and Face.

♊ Arms

♌ Heart

♎ Reins

♐ Thighs

♒ Legs

♉ Neck

♋ Breast

♍ Bowels

♏ Secrets

♑ Knees

♓ The Feet.

To find where the sign is.

First find the Day of the Month, and against the Day you have the Sign or Place of the Moon in the 6th Column. Then finding the sign there, it shews the Part of the body it governs.

MAN's head and face Heaven's ram obey,
His neck the neck-strong bull does sway,
The arm-twining twins guides hands and arms;
Breasts, sides and stomach *Cancer* charms,
The lion rules his back and heart,
Bowels and belly's *Virgo*'s part;
Reins, haunches, navel, *Libra* tends,
Bladder and Secrets *Scorpio*, befriends:
The half-hors'd bowman rules the thighs,
And to the kid our knees suffice;
Our legs are but the butler's fees,
The fish our footsteps oversees.

The lion rules his back and heart
Bowels and belly's Virgo's part
Veins, haunches, navel, Libra tends
Bladder and secrets Scorpio befriends
The half-hors'd bowman rules the thighs,
And to the goat our knees suffice
Our legs are but the butler's fees
The fish our footsteps oversees.

The idea that groups of stars called constellations influence parts of the body or human events is ancient. It probably started thousands of years ago with the first stargazers. Some early astronomers thought they had discovered a relationship between the motions of heavenly bodies and human events on Earth. This early kind of thinking was called astrology. Over the centuries with the rise of modern science and astronomy, astrology has come to be known as a pseudo-science.

It is interesting to note that in recent years there has been a renewed interest in astrology. Many newspapers carry a daily horoscope. Find a horoscope in a newspaper and compare it with the one in Banneker's almanac. Your newspaper horoscope will probably show the calendar year divided into twelve parts with a sign or constellation governing each part. Some astrologers claim to be able to predict and guide the events of a person's life by using the sign or constellation under which he or she is born.

Benjamin Banneker became famous in his time for the astronomical calculations presented in his almanacs. But he was more than a successful, self-taught scientist. Although he was free, he was aware of and deeply bothered by slavery and the treatment received by his people in America. Restrictions were being used to oppress free blacks as well as slaves. During the last four years of Banneker's life, he could not vote. Some whites were beginning to fear free, educated blacks more than slaves. Banneker was one of the early black Americans to speak out for the cause of racial equality and the abolition of slavery.

He also was concerned about the attitudes of public officials toward the plight and abilities of his race in America. He sent a handwritten copy of his first almanac to Thomas Jefferson. Jefferson, the author of the Declaration of Independence, was himself a slave owner. Along with the copy of his almanac, Banneker sent a letter to Jefferson, dated August 19, 1791, in which he wrote:

We are a race of beings who have long labored under the abuse and censure of the world. . . . We have long been considered rather as brutish than human, and scarcely capable of mental endowments.

Sir, I hope . . . that you are a man far less inflexible in sentiments of this nature than many others, that you are measurably friendly and well disposed toward us. . . .

Now sir . . . . I apprehend that your sentiments are concurrent with mine, which are that our universal Father hath given being to all. . . .

But, Sir, how pitiable it is to reflect that, although you were so fully convinced of the benevolence of the Father of mankind . . . . That you should at the same time counteract His mercies in detaining by fraud and violence so numerous a part of my brethren under groaning captivity and cruel oppression. . . .

Suffer me, Sir, to recall . . . that when the tyranny of the British crown was exerted to reduce you to servitude, your abhorrence was so excited that you publicly held forth this true and invaluable doctrine . . . . 'We hold these truths to be self-evident, that all men are created equal, and that they are endowed by their Creator with certain inalienable rights; that among these are life, liberty, and pursuit of happiness'. . . .

The Almanac is a production of my arduous study. I have long had unbounded desires to become acquainted with the secrets of nature, and I have had to gratify my curiosity herein through my own assiduous application to astronomical study. I need not recount to you the many difficulties and disadvantages I have had to encounter. I conclude by subscribing myself, with the most profound respect, your most humble servant,

B. Banneker

This letter made Jefferson uncomfortable and it also impressed him. He sent the almanac to his friend Condorcet, the Secretary of the Academy of Sciences in Paris, to prove that the color of a man's skin was no bar to brains: "I am happy to inform you that we have now in the United States a Negro . . . who is a very respectable mathematician," he wrote to Condorcet. And to Banneker he wrote the following letter in reply:

Sir, I thank you sincerely for your letter, and for the Almanac it contained. Nobody wishes more than I do to see such proofs as you exhibit that nature has given to our black brethren talents equal to those of the other colors of men, and that the appearance of want of them is owning only to the degraded condition of their existence both in Africa and America. I can add, with truth, that no one wishes more ardently to see a good system commenced for raising the condition both of their body and mind, to what it ought to be, as fast as the imbecility of their present existence, and other circumstances which cannot be neglected, will admit. I have taken the liberty of sending your almanac to Monsieur Condorcet, Secretary of the Academy of Sciences at Paris, and to members of the Philanthropic Society, because I considered it a document to which your whole color had a right, for their justification against the doubts which have been entertained of them. I am, with great esteem, sir, your most obedient servant,

Thomas Jefferson

With his almanac, Benjamin Banneker was pleased that he was able to do something to help the cause for his oppressed race, by proving that nature had given black people great mental abilities as well as physical.

After 1802, Banneker was too old and feeble to continue the calculation of almanacs. He died in 1806, and was buried near the cabin that had been his lifetime home and the place where he carried out all of his scientific work.

The *Federal Gazette* and *Baltimore Daily Advertiser*, dated October 28, 1806, printed the following death announcement:

On Sunday, the 25th instant, departed this life, near his residence in Baltimore County, Mr. Benjamin Banneker, a black man, immediate descendant of an African father. He was known in this neighborhood for his quiet and peaceful demeanor and among scientific men, as an astronomer and mathematician.

THE MEANING
OF BANNEKER'S LIFE AND WORKS

Benjamin Banneker was more than a self-taught mathematician, astronomer, surveyor, poet, and mechanic. He was also a humanitarian. He cared intensely about the quality of life for black people in America. He spoke out boldly in his letters and conversations with the nation's leaders for the humane treatment of his people. He showed to a slave-holding nation that blacks are a part of the human family. He used his own achievements as proof that the idea of the inferiority of black people of African descent should be destroyed. His life was a search for independence, just as it was for the American colonies during the 1700's and the Revolutionary War.

Nine years before Banneker died, this epitaph appeared in his almanac for 1797.

Epitaph for a Watch-Maker
Here lies, in a horizontal position,
    The outside case of
    Peter Pendulum, Watch-Maker
Whose abilities in that line were an honour
    To his profession.
    Integrity was the main spring
      And prudence was the regulator
      Of all the actions of his life.
    Humane, generous and liberal
      His hand never stopped
      Till he had relieved distress
So nicely regulated were all his motions
    That he never went wrong
    Except when set a-going
      By people
    Who did not know
      His key!
    Even then he was easily
      Set right again.
He had the art of disposing his time
      So well,
    That his hours glided away,
      In one continual round
      Of pleasures and delights
Till an unlucky minute put a period to
      His existence.

He departed this life
  Wound up
In hope of being taken in hand
  By his Maker
And of being thoroughly cleaned, repaired,
    And set a-going
  In the world to come.

CHARLES HENRY TURNER

1867–1923

He Studied the Behavior of Insects

He was lying flat on the ground watching some ants. His stomach was pressed against the bare brown earth. His eyes were only a few inches from the dirt. The ants were very busy. One by one they moved in and out of their tiny hole in the ground. They seemed to know exactly where they were going. Some of the ants would take long trips away from the ant hill around the hole, always finding their way home without getting lost. How mysterious all this was, thought Charles H. Turner, his eyes fixed intently on the ants moving around the hole. The movements of the ants fascinated him, particularly their sense of direction. Their actions almost seemed human.

How were the ants able to find their way back to the nest? The ant hole leading into the underground home was only slightly larger than the period at the end of this sentence. Surely, thought young Turner, ants couldn't see the hole as clearly as he saw it from above.

As a young boy, Charles was always asking questions about nature. He wondered how or why an animal acts the way it does. He was especially interested in small animals crawling and flying about. Constantly he asked his teachers questions about the small creatures he saw. One day his teacher replied, "If you want to know all of those things about them, why don't you go and find out for yourself?" Charles Turner answered, "I will."

Charles H. Turner spent his life-time searching for answers to his many questions about animal behavior. In doing so he became one of the great scientists of this century. He made first-time discoveries about the behavior of bees, moths, ants, cockroaches, and many other insects.

Between 1892 and 1923, Charles H. Turner had forty-nine scientific articles accepted for publication. These articles, reporting his experiments, discoveries, and ideas about animal behavior appeared in the leading scientific journals of his time, such as the *Biological Bulletin*, the *Journal of Comparative Neurology*, *Zoological Bulletin*, the *Journal of Animal Behavior* and the *Psychological Bulletin*. His works appeared under such titles as "Psychological Notes on the Gallery Spider," "Habits of Mound-Building Ants," "Behavior of a Parasitic Bee," "Hunting Habits of an American Sand Wasp," and "Do Ants Form Practical Judgment?" The quality and quantity of Dr. Turner's work was amazing.

His scientific work was studied and highly regarded by scientists in America and Europe. Dozens of quotations from his published articles were found in important books of the day on animal behavior. Some of these books were: *Wheeler's Ant Book*, *The Animal Mind*, by Washburn, *Mind in Animals* by Smith, and *The Psychic Life of Insects*, by Bouvier, a French scientist. Here is a section taken from *The Animal Mind*, by Washburn:

Recently C. H. Turner has come to the conclusion that ants are not guided 'slavishly' or reflexly by the odor of their tracks in finding the way to and from the nest. He made a small cardboard stage from which an inclined cardboard bridge led down to the artificial ant nest. Ants and pupae were placed on the stage. After the ants had, through random movements, learned the way down the incline a second incline was placed so as to lead from the opposite side of the stage to the nest. No ants went down this way. The inclines were then exchanged so that the one bearing the scent of the ant's footprints was on the opposite side and the unscented incline in the old place; the ants continued to go down in the old place. . . . He

(Turner) confirms Bethe's observation that the pathways to and from the nest are different, but does not find that even a single ant follows her own footsteps in both directions. The direction of the light, not the smell, is the ruling factor in pathfinding, according to Turner, who offers the following experimental evidence. . . .

In the animal behavior literature of France a certain characteristic ant movement was given the name of its discoverer, Dr. Turner. The movement was called "Turner's circling." It refers to a peculiar turning movement, taken by some ants as they find their way home to a nest, as observed and described by Dr. Turner.

Dr. Turner was born in 1867 in Cincinnati, Ohio, where he attended elementary school and graduated from high school. His father was a church custodian; his mother was a practical nurse. It has been said that his father was a keen thinker, with an intense thirst for knowledge. He acquired a large home library of several hundred books. One of Charles' earliest ambitions was to learn to read his father's books.

In 1891, Charles H. Turner earned a Bachelor of Science degree and in 1892 a Master of Science degree, both from the University of Cincinnati. He taught in the biological laboratories at the University of Cincinnati for a brief time before moving on to other positions.

Charles H. Turner could have devoted all of his time and energies to scientific research. However, he chose a different path—teaching fulltime and carrying on his research when he wasn't in the classroom with his pupils. Although he did go on to earn a doctorate degree in science, he never held a teaching position at any large American university with outstanding research facilities.

He was committed to helping to educate his own people, especially its youth. His commitment is perhaps reflected in this letter he wrote to Booker T. Washington, head of Tuskegee Institute, in Alabama, in 1893.

BIOLOGICAL LABORATORY
University of Cincinnati

April 29, 1893

Prof. Booker T. Washington,

Dear Sir:

I am a colored man and at present am teaching in the University of Cincinnati (white). I am anxious to get to work among my own people. I would like to obtain a position as Professor of Natural History. Miss A.G. Baldwin informed me that you might know of an opening. Enclosed you will find copies of two letters of recommendation etc. I can furnish several such at any time. Hoping to hear from you I am

Very truly,

C. H. Turner

In 1893, Charles Turner went to Clark University in Atlanta, Georgia, as a professor of biology. From then to 1907, he held several different positions in education, from teacher to high school principal to college instructor in science. During this period of time, Turner carried out experiments on spiders, crayfish, ants, and many other invertebrates (animals without backbones). Most of his research was done alone and unaided. For his pioneering work and his original discoveries and contributions to the field of animal behavior, he was awarded a Doctor of Philosophy degree in 1907 from the University of Chicago. For a black American in the early 1900's this was an outstanding achievement.

On June 5, 1906, a hand-written letter of application for a teaching position was received by the principal of Sumner High School in St. Louis, Missouri. The letter was signed—C. H. Turner. With this letter came this statement from the minister of Turner's church: "Charles H. Turner is a member in good and regular standing. . . . a scientist by nature and training."

And so, in November, 1908, Dr. Charles H. Turner became a teacher of biology at Sumner High School. His starting salary was $1,080 per year. He moved his family from Augusta, Georgia, to St. Louis.

In her later years, Dr. Turner's daughter recalled that she and her brothers grew up in a highly scientific atmosphere, both in Georgia and St. Louis. They were accustomed to living with many books and laboratory specimens of ants, bees, roaches, snakes, and other creatures. These things kept his children interested in and curious about animal life and behavior. "My father to us," she said, "was just a plain, kind man who instilled in us those qualities that would make for the simple, successful life."

DR. TURNER—THE TEACHER

As a new teacher at Sumner High School in 1908, Dr. Turner had taken the place of the previous biology teacher, Mr. Clark. Some of the students in the senior class were curious to get a look at Mr. Clark's replacement, so a small group of them flocked to Dr. Turner's room to study.

Not knowing this new teacher's name, the class president decided he would find it out by asking. Dr. Turner erased some writing from the chalkboard and wrote his name. The president proceeded to read aloud: "Dr. C. H. Turner, inorganic, not living matter." This, of course, brought laughter from the students. Dr. Turner smiled. The last phrase—inorganic, not living matter— was a portion of the writing that Dr. Turner had not erased from the chalkboard.

Dr. Turner taught biology and psychology at Sumner High School from 1908 until the time of his death in 1923. His lectures and courses were far from being non-living and inorganic. His students were impressed by the wealth of live animals and plants he collected for study and experimentation. He acquired the most modern scientific instruments for his students. His lessons frequently required the use of microscopes. He clarified his lectures using colored chalk to draw exciting illustrations. Often he would draw the illustrations on the board using both hands at the same time.

Dr. Turner was a completely dedicated teacher. The welfare and development of his students was always foremost in his mind. Whenever he was not out in the field alone observing and experimenting, he would be out there with his students. Often he would take boys on long hikes through the woods, stimulating in them a curiosity about nature and a reverence for life. He lifted his students into other worlds as they looked at nature through his eyes and mind. He translated the "coos" of pigeons' talk into their expressions of love, home planning, and family life. It seemed as if Dr. Turner fully understood the language of birds.

Dr. Turner was an outstanding research scientist. He was also an outstanding and inspiring teacher. He brought a wealth of first-hand information about the behavior of living things to his classroom talks. His information was based on research that he carried on in his spare time during the school year and during the summer months when insects and other living creatures were flourishing.

The notes below are excerpts taken from the biology notebook of a student of Dr. Turner's in 1909:

ANTS

If you dig in an ant city when all kinds are present you will find several kinds.

Bachelor ants or drones are ants that are quite graceful, having two pairs of wings. They are more or less slender in shape and are the laziest ants known and are stupid; they never work but are always loafing up and down the city and if they stray from home there is no way for them to get back unless they are carried by another ant.

The young maiden or queen ant has two pairs of wings and is usually larger than the male but is not lazy like the male. She can do any kind of work. Only once in the life of the ant can the maiden fly or use her wings, and that is on her bridal tour.

That night or soon after the wedding the bachelor ant dies. After the death of the bachelor ant, the widow comes to the surface of the ground and breaks off her wings. She has no more use for them since she never marries again.

Workers are old maid ants. They never marry. They are born from eggs laid by a mother ant. They hatch into a baby young maiden ant without arms, legs, wings, antennae, or eyes. They must be carried, washed, fed, and carried out to air by the mother ant. Everything must be done for them. At one point in its development it stops eating and begins to spin a thread-like cocoon. Once wrapped in the cocoon it grows into an adult with appendages. . . .

Habits of Ants

The toilet habits of ants are especially commendable. They are very clean. They clean themselves and their friends. On their appendages they have a comb and brush. The jaws are used to clean with also. Ants always have a dump pile where all undesired or refuse matter is placed. This dump pile is also their grave yard.

⊢ Here is a diagram showing ants moving abreast for a
| | funeral procession. Each alternate couple takes a dead
⊢ ant and goes to the dumping ground. The alternate
| | couples dug the grave. Two ants did not take part in the
⊢ funeral exercises. . . .

Behavior of Bees

Homing of Bees—Dr. Turner's experiment on mining bees. One morning on his way to school, Dr. Turner noticed a hole in the earth. Next to the hole was a Coca Cola bottle cap. A bee passed by and dropped into the hole. The bee came out of the hole and flew away, but returned in about 20 minutes. The bee was collecting pollen from flowers in the field and storing it in an underground burrow. While the bee was afield, Dr. Turner made a hole in the earth with a stick and then placed the bottle cap next to the hole he made. When the bee returned from the field, the new hole was entered, but the bee came out immediately. She circled around and found her own hole and dropped into it. She soon came out again and was gone for 30 minutes. Dr. Turner made several more holes with the stick and placed Coca Cola bottle caps beside each hole. When the bee returned she was confused. She could not find the right hole. The bee found her own hole only after hunting around and entering the wrong holes and finding they were not her home. These experiments showed that bees relied on memory of the surroundings around the hole to find its home. . . .

Bees have the ability to tell time. In 1907, three times a day from 7–9, 12–2, and 5–7, the table was set with jam in dishes.

> The bees appeared at the table at all three meals. Then Dr. Turner put jam only at breakfast daily. They still came to each meal but found no jam at noon and night. Soon they stopped coming. This shows they have some idea of time. . . .

Dr. Turner was an unusual scientist. To find the truth about why and how animals behave as they do and to share his observations and discoveries with his students was of the greatest importance to him. He believed that the best possible way in which his discoveries could be used was to enrich the lives of young boys and girls.

Once, during an after-class conversation, one of Dr. Turner's students asked him why he chose to teach in a high school when he had been offered a professorship at the University of Chicago. This was at a time when few blacks were even admitted to large universities, much less sought as instructors. Dr. Turner's reply to his student's query was this: "I feel that I am needed here and can do so much more for my people."

After the death of Dr. Charles H. Turner, the St. Louis Board of Education erected a school for the physically handicapped. The school was named the Charles H. Turner School. In 1954, when this school for physically handicapped black children was combined with that for white children, the building was converted to a school for seventh and eighth grades. Today the Turner Middle School in St. Louis stands in memory of one of its greatest teachers and an outstanding scientist.

DR. TURNER—THE SCIENTIST

Although Dr. Charles H. Turner was a biology teacher from 1908 until his death, he was best known among scientists for his research work. He was known by the some fifty research papers he had published on neurology, invertebrate ecology, and animal behavior. In addition to his research reports, he was asked to write reviews of the literature on comparative psychology in the *Psychological Bulletin* and in the *Journal of Animal Behavior*.

The science of animal behavior deals with the actions of a single animal and of animals in groups. This is not an easy thing to study. At the heart of this science is describing what an animal does and then deciding if the action is important. In other sciences, like chemistry and physics, scientists have a pretty good idea of what they want to observe and describe or measure. But in animal behavior the scientist must approach his animal with an open mind in deciding which actions to record.

Dr. Turner's most productive work was his many series of investigations on the behavior of insects, including some unusual experimental techniques. He spent much time thinking about his method of experimenting before he went out into the field. He built some ingenious devices, some simple and some intricate, to help him solve some of the big problems of animal behavior. For example, by using the apparatus shown on the following page, Dr. Turner discovered that light-rays as landmarks played a larger factor than had previously been thought in helping ants to find their way home.

The stage or platform in the center of the apparatus illustration was made of cardboard. Using a narrow cardboard inclined plane (P) Dr. Turner could connect the stage to a nest (O) of ants. To the right and left of the stage were electric lights (B). The lights were arranged so

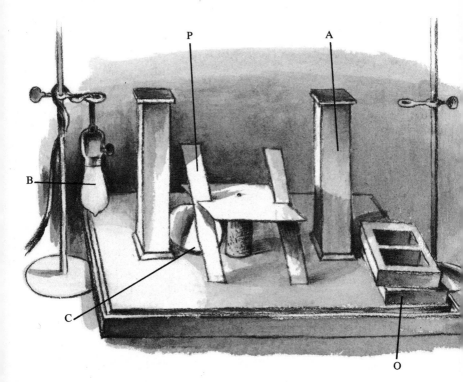

The device shown above was built by Turner and used in conducting light-ray experiments with ants.

that when the light on one side was burning the other automatically shut off. The lights were separated from the stage by heat filters (A). A mirror (C) was used for viewing ants crawling on the lower side of the inclined plane.

Dr. Turner placed a number of ants with their eggs, larvae, and pupae upon the stage, and then switched on the light on the right side of the stage. Soon a procession of ants passed to and fro between the nest and the stage along the inclined plane on the right side. Then Dr. Turner attached a second plane to the left side of the stage. He now had one incline on the side where the light was shining and another on the opposite side. The ants continued to travel along the pathway on the right. After the ants had been using the lighted right side for several hours, he switched off the light on the right and turned on the light on the left. "Immediately a remark-able change occurs," said Dr. Turner. "The ants act as though they were in a panic. They seemed lost," he re-ported. Within an hour the ants were using the plane on the left side to enter and leave the stage. Dr. Turner interpreted this result by saying—"Evidently light is a factor in guiding these ants home."

In his work on the homing of the burrowing bees, Dr. Turner spent from five to ten hours a day during the month of August, 1908, studying these insects in the field. This made it possible for him to conduct several series of experiments. He was interested in comparing the method used by the burrowing bees to find their way home with those used by ants and wasps. At the time of his experimentation with the bees, some scientists be-lieved that bees were guided home by sun rays and wind.

The bee homing experiments were carried out in a deserted garden, and were performed upon a bee that occupied a burrow all to itself. Dr. Turner explained the way in which he determined how many bees occupied a burrow like this: "I would plug the opening (entrance to the burrow) and then observe it carefully for an hour or longer. The bees, on returning, would circle about the nest. After a while they would usually try to dig around the plug. By counting the bees that appeared and tarried, it was easy to determine how many bees were occupying the burrow. When the required information was obtained, the plug was removed."

The burrow was situated in a small barren spot and surrounded by a few blades of grass, which partially covered the opening. Before the first three experiments were done, Dr. Turner had observed a bee arrive at 9:35 a.m. and immediately enter the burrow. At 9:37 a.m., it departed again for the field. The bee was making twenty-minute trips to flowers in the field for pollen, which it was storing in the burrow. This is how Turner described some of the twenty experiments he carried out during the Summer. Following each one are his recorded observations:

Experiment 1

While the bee was afield, a rectangular piece of white paper, 12 cm. by 8 cm., in the center of which was a hole 13 mm. in diameter was so adjusted over the nest as to have the hole in the paper coincide with the opening of the burrow.

At 9:55 a.m., the bee arrived with its burden of pollen. Instead of entering the nest, it circled around and around. It then hovered momentarily over the white rectangle and then described yet wider circles in the air. At 9:57 a.m., two minutes after its return from the field, the bee entered the nest. On again departing for the field, at 10:00 a.m., the bee hovered a while above the paper that surrounded the nest; then after making several turns of a helicoid (spiral) curve, flew away.

Experiment 2

The same conditions as in experiment one.

At 10:20 a.m., the bee arrived from its trip, hovered for less than half a minute and then dropped into the nest. At 10:24 a.m., the bee departed, without stopping to explore the surroundings of the nest.

Experiment 3

About four inches to the east of the nest opening, a hole was made in the ground. Over this hole was placed the piece of white paper, with the hole in the center, which was adjusted over the nest in experiment two. A piece of watermelon rind, with a thirteen mm. hole in the center, was so adjusted over the nest as to have the hole in the rind coincide with the opening of the burrow. One-half of the rind was brown, the other half yellowish-green; the line dividing these two colors bisected the hole in the center of the rind.

At 10:47 a.m., the bee arrived with its burden of pollen. It hovered above the watermelon rind for a moment, then circled about the place. At 10:48 a.m., after a search of one minute, the bee entered the nest. On leaving the nest at 10:59 a.m., the bee examined carefully the surroundings before departing.

Experiment 4

While the bee was afield, the piece of watermelon rind was removed and a rectangular piece of white paper, 8 cm. long and 5 cm. wide, was arched over the nest in such a way as to form a tent 6 cm. high, the east and west ends of which were open. The rectangular piece of white paper, with the hole in the center, which was left in the same position as in Experiment 3, was situated just in front of the eastern opening of the tent.

When the bee arrived, at 11:15 a.m., it circled about for two minutes (until 11:17 a.m.) and then dropped into the hole over which the rectangular piece of paper, with the hole in its center, had been adjusted. It emerged at once and, after circling about for a short time, reentered the hole. It emerged immediately. Finally at 11:18 a.m., three minutes after arriving on the spot, the bee entered the tent, through the eastern opening, and dropped into the burrow. On emerging from the nest at 11:31 a.m., the bee hovered a moment inside of the tent. It then passed out of the east opening and hovered for a few seconds above the tent. Then, keeping close to the top of the grass, it flew about for a while in a sub-helicoidal curve and then flew away to the field.

As a result of these experiments, Dr. Turner concluded that burrowing bees are guided by memory in finding the way home. They examine carefully the neighborhood of the nest for the purpose of forming memory pictures of the land surface (topography) around the burrow. Any change in the topography seemed to confuse the bee upon its return to find the entrance to its home.

Can The Honey Bee Distinguish Colors?

Another question that Dr. Turner wanted to answer was this: what attracts insects to flowers—the sweet odor or the color of the flowers? For many years other scientists had been trying to learn if bees could see colors and if colors guided them to flowers. The results of the various experiments were often contradictory.

During the summer of 1910, Dr. Turner carried out some experiments in O'Fallon Park in St. Louis. Using his ever ingenious methods, he designed tests with colored disks of paper and colored boxes which were filled with honey. He found that odors alone did not lead bees to flowers. Based on his findings he believed that bees responded to colors in many ways and further-more, that they were capable of recognizing them at a great distance.

At the end of his research paper entitled *Experiments on Color-Vision of the Honey Bee*, published by the famous Marine Biological Laboratory at Woods Hole, Massachusetts, Dr. Turner said the following: "These experiments prove that, to the bee, my colored disks, my colored cornucopias, and my colored boxes were something more than mere sensations. It seems to me that they were true percepts ... those strange red things had come to mean 'honey-bearers,' and those strange green things and strange blue things had come to mean 'not honey-bearers.' Hence, whenever the bees saw the red things, they made the appropriate movements for securing the honey, and when they saw the blue things or the green things they passed on. . . ." (Dr. Turner did not mean however, that bees preferred red rather than blue or green, or that they saw red as humans do.)

In November, 1910, another scientist, J. H. Lovell published an article resulting from research he had done. Lovell's article was titled "The Color Sense of the Honey Bee; Can Bees Distinguish Colors." Dr. Lovell used an experimental method that was quite different from Dr. Turner's, yet Lovell's results led him to form the same conclusions as Turner's.

Can The Honey Bee Distinguish Between Patterns?

Dr. Turner was not content with discovering that bees were capable of sensing colors. A year later he carried out in great detail a series of experiments that proved that bees could distinguish between patterns. Here, too, he used ingeniously devised paper boxes with various color markings. The paper boxes served as artificial flowers.

His method was to encourage a few bees to learn that they could collect honey more easily from artificial flowers of a certain color pattern than they could from real flowers. After the bees had thoroughly learned this, he tried to find out if the bees could select the artificial flowers with this particular color pattern from a number of different color patterns. The result of this investigation was the discovery that bees can distinguish color patterns. Dr. Turner believed that this ability was of value to bees in recognizing plants that yield honey.

"Playing Possum"

All of Dr. Turner's work did not involve experimentation. Sometimes he would just sit for hours and observe the actions of insects. The behavior of a marvel of the insect world, the pit-making ant-lion, was one of his favorite insects to study.

He described in detail the ant-lion's method of excavating a pit in the ground. When the pit was complete it served as a trap for other insects. He explained the method the creature used in capturing prey, which it sucked dry with its hollow jaws.

With painstaking experiments, Dr. Turner worked out the details of the insect's ability to "play possum." He concluded that when the insect suddenly "played dead" this was its way of reacting when startled. When the ant-lion lies motionless for prolonged periods of time, Dr. Turner said, "It is really not feigning death at all, and requires no self-command. It is simply terror paralysis which has become so useful that it has become hereditary."

Can a Cockroach Learn?

Dr. Turner did some important work with the common cockroach. In a paper entitled "Behavior of the Common Roach on an Open Maze," he found that a roach could be taught within a day to run a maze. The roach learned by trial and error, but in doing so also used sense stimuli.

In another study he worked with roaches that were nocturnal and habitually shunned the light. He trained them to reverse their lifelong habit and avoid the dark instead. This was done by teaching them to avoid certain dark places. Every time the roach approached a dark place it would receive an electric shock from a device contrived by Dr. Turner. He found that male roaches seemed to learn more quickly than the females, and that young roaches were more apt at learning than adult roaches.

Can Insects Hear?

During Dr. Turner's time most naturalists believed that insects could hear, but this had never been proved experimentally. Scientists simply thought that since insects could produce sounds, then other members of the species could hear them. Dr. Turner proved that a certain kind of moth could not only hear sounds, but also sounds of a certain pitch. He demonstrated this with an organ pipe and a Galton whistle. Moreover, he discovered that a species which responds only to a high pitch on the Galton whistle can be taught to respond to low tones when the low tones mean danger to the insect.

Scientists and nature lovers were grateful for Dr. Turner's contributions. In his studies he did not venture on lengthy and costly trips to far-away places. He had the ability to take the material that was near at hand and make the most of it.

The handicaps under which Dr. Turner's work was accomplished were many. They were modestly and bravely met. One of these was the limitation of a small salary, out of which he had to purchase his own scientific equipment, materials, and library of books for research. He did not enjoy the use of elaborate college research laboratories and institutions available to many professional scientists.

DR. TURNER—THE MAN

Dr. Turner's interests were not solely scientific. Among his unfinished papers were found several chapters of a novel, a number of chapters of a book of nature stories for children, and the manuscript of a book of thirty-two poems.

Often he spent time and energy working for the civil rights and betterment of life of his people in St. Louis. He pioneered in developing social service work among black people there. In 1923, not only did science lose one of its most thorough and productive students, but black people lost one of their most efficient workers.

On May 25, 1923, a memorial service for Dr. Charles H. Turner was held in the auditorium of Sumner High School, in St. Louis, Missouri. Many people who had known Dr. Turner spoke of him that day to the student body of Sumner High. One of the speakers was Mr. A. G. Pohlman, who came to represent the Academy of Science of St. Louis. Here is Mr. Pohlman's memorial speech, read to the students and faculty gathered together that day:

CHARLES HENRY TURNER
An Appreciation

It has been said that the size of a man may be measured in terms of his influence for good and for the betterment of his fellow man. But just as the striving to attain is more important to us than the desired thing itself, so we tend to look abroad for a truly great man when, forsooth, he walks in our very midst. We are very likely to think of the great man as one who has acquired a vast amount of money; as one who has gained social prominence; as one whose opinion on public questions is eagerly sought. Many people mistake notoriety for fame; confuse the word politician for statesman; take for granted that the well-known is the equivalent for great. Were not these historians so overcome with the pomp and the splendor of a Pilate that they quite forgot to mention the humble Carpenter of Nazareth? It may be well to consider some of the features which go to make up the truly great man, that those of us who have sought afar shall recognize a brother who perhaps at this moment is touching elbows with us.

The first essential in the great man is a devotion to work. Some of us envy the well-known man who toils but little and therein we cater to our own ambitions of lassitude. But no man is great unless he rises above the petty inconveniences of his surroundings. No man is strong unless he meets the competition about him. Devotion to work means exactly what it says. It does not mean devotion to methods. It does not imply a certain number of hours a day. It does not suggest a contentment with the doing of a daily stint in a manner which calls for neither commendation or criticism. Devotion to work means work because one must work, and, faced by such a spirit, seemingly insurmountable obstacles are swept away along with trivial factors of birth and race and station.

But work itself is not enough. The second ingredient in our strength of character is unselfishness: the desire to share the joys and sorrows of life with others; the accomplishment of the friendly act for its own sake; the appreciation of a bond of proper sympathy of man for man. The man who works with unselfish devotion ever searches for that which shall bring his neighbor to a higher level of doing and thinking and living. A great man must indeed be unselfish and take pride in the merit which his talent may lend others.

And in the search for truth, even in the little things of life, our great man interprets that which he finds and is ever threading the beads of fact into some pattern of a worldly philosophy. Faithfulness to truth is after all a faithfulness to the little things, and our great man achieves merit in his respect for that which is known and that which in unknown. Because of his consciousness of his own limitations and because of his respect for truth, the great man is humble.

We have been misinformed in our ideas of great men. We have been misled into looking for magnificence and for vain-glorious trappings in which our fancy would clothe an important person. Indeed the humble simplicity of the truly great man disarms us quite completely and we crane the neck to overlook exactly that which we seek.

It is for you who knew Doctor Turner to satisfy yourself that here indeed was a great man. It is for you to determine in your own hearts if this man possessed the strength of character, the devotion to work, the faithfulness to ideals, the respect for truth, and the unselfishness in sharing that which he possessed. Was he indeed the humble man of science who might well be taken into the fold of the most highly esteemed?

You have answered this question yourselves. It will not be given to many of us that men and women and little children shall gather together after we are gone to pay tribute to our memory. It is a privilege to appear before you as a representative of the Academy of Science, an organization of which Dr. Turner was not only a member, but also a councilor. Let each one of you cherish the memory of Dr. Turner, who left behind him the priceless heritage of devoted service that those who knew him and worked with him cannot help but have been the better and the stronger through his contact.

Permit me, in the name of the Academy of Science, to pay our respect not only to Turner the Scientist, but also to Turner the Man.

ERNEST E. JUST

1883–1941

He Studied the Eggs of Marine Animals

On the evening of February 12, 1915, the Governor of New York stood on the stage at Ethical Culture Hall in New York City. In his hand was a gold medal. It was the Spingarn Medal to be awarded for the first time ever, "to the man or woman of African descent and American citizenship who shall have made the highest achievement during the preceding year or years in any honorable field of human endeavor." On the stage behind the Governor sat his staff and the officials of the National Association for the Advancement of Colored People (NAACP). Each year, except one, since 1915, the NAACP has presented this award. In recent years the medal has been given to such people as Sammy Davis, Jr., Edward W. Brooke, and Clarence Mitchell.

The man who was to receive the first Spingarn Medal was not a social reformer. He had not made any great speeches for the equality of black Americans. He had not led any successful protest movements for the civil rights of his people. Ernest E. Just was being recognized for his work as a pure scientist. He had been carrying out pioneering investigations on the nature of animal cells, and was a brilliant investigator of the living cell, especially the egg cells of marine animals. He had earned the reputation of being a "scientist's scientist." Dr. Charles Drew, whose work is discussed in Chapter One, called Dr. Just "a biologist of unusual skill and the greatest of our original thinkers in the field."

Everyone was glad to be at the Ethical Culture Hall that evening, except Ernest E. Just. He wished he could have been working in his laboratory, teaching a group of students, or at home reading—anywhere but on a stage in front of an audience who would listen to speeches praising him and then clap. He hated publicity. This was a very embarassing evening for the young scientist, and in fact, he had even tried to prevent it. He had written to the officials of the NAACP to say that he was disturbed over being the winner of the award for 1914. In a letter to the secretary of the NAACP he wrote: "My contributions have been meager. It rather upsets me to learn that I am expected to be present at the award ceremony, doubtless in the presence of a large audience. I feel deeply that I ought not court publicity, since courtship ought to be incompatible with scientific endeavor." Despite his modesty and dislike for so much attention being given his work as a scientist, the medal could not be denied him.

When Ernest Just stepped forward to receive the Spingarn Medal from the Governor, he whispered a "thank-you" and shrank back into his seat. He appreciated the honor and was filled with more determination to achieve through his work as a research biologist. And indeed he did go on to achieve. He went on to work and study with some of the greatest minds in 20th century biology, at one of the most famous research laboratories in this country and at others in Germany, France, and Italy.

In thirty-five years of the most productive and critical research, Ernest Just added new information and ideas about the structure and workings of the living cell. And, as you will see, although Just was modest and quiet about his scientific work and thinking, he was not afraid to challenge the scientific theories of some of the great biologists of the nineteenth and twentieth centuries.

In 1916, Ernest E. Just received his doctorate degree from the University of Chicago for his studies of animal reproduction. In later years other distinguished biologists voted that a star be placed by his name in *American Men of Science.* The star meant that his fellow scientists thought of him as a leader in the field of biological science. Dr. Just, during his lifetime, wrote and had published over sixty papers describing his experiments, and two books, *Basic Methods for Experiments in Eggs of Marine Animals* and *The Biology of the Cell Surface.*

In the 1920's and 1930's, Dr. Just perhaps knew more about the egg cells of marine animals and their development into new life than any biologist of his time. The cell is the basic living part of all living things. Live cells contain a complex mixture of elements and compounds. The interaction of the hundreds of substances produces living material as we know it. One of the frontiers of science today is the possibility of man-made creation of a living substance or a cell. It is only because of the pioneering work of scientists like Dr. Just that today's scientists are getting closer to knowing how "to create life in a test tube." As science advances it builds on the knowledge left by the great thinkers of the past. Ernest E. Just was one of the first to unlock the secrets of cell reproduction and to present new theories of cell life.

Most animals that you are familiar with (and also humans) started life as single cells. This original cell came from the joining of two specialized cells from the parents of the new animal. When a sperm cell from the father parent meets an egg cell from the mother and joins with it to form one cell, a new life begins. The joining of a sperm and an egg cell is called fertilization. The fertilized egg then begins to divide into more cells and is known as an embryo. Eventually, after thousands of cell divisions, the embryo develops into a full-grown animal, made up of millions of cells in some cases.

THE ROAD TO ACHIEVEMENT

It is important to note that in 1915, as the first Spingarn medalist, Ernest Just was only thirty-two years old. It had only been eight years before that he had graduated from Dartmouth College.

Dartmouth College, the Ivy League school in Hanover, New Hampshire, is quite a way from Charleston, South Carolina. Ernest Just was born in this southern city in 1883. His father, a builder of wharves, died when Ernest was four years old. His mother was a teacher, who guided her son's early childhood education. At seventeen, after finishing his public schooling at a school for black students in Orangeburg, South Carolina, young Just left his birthplace and headed north for more and better education.

Ernest Just spent his first summer away from home working in New York. He earned enough money to take him even further north to Kimball Academy in New Hampshire. Kimball Academy was a four-year prep school that prepared boys for college. At Kimball, Ernest Just was placed in the lowest class despite the fact that he had already spent six years in school in Orangeburg. But his schooling in South Carolina really hadn't prepared him for college, so four more years of high school lay ahead of him. A college education was foremost in his mind. He dug hard into his studies and finished four years' work at Kimball in three years.

Just was an excellent student and made a brilliant record. His teachers at Kimball recommended that he go to Dartmouth College, not far from Kimball. With scholarship aid and loans, he was able to begin his college studies at Dartmouth.

At Dartmouth Just was interested in only one thing— preparing himself for his life's work. At first college life wasn't what he thought it would be. During his freshman year he often thought that perhaps he was in the wrong place. It seemed that all anyone ever talked about or cared about at Dartmouth was football. The rivalry between Dartmouth and Harvard gripped the campus. A freshman who was not out at every game rooting for the team was frowned upon. As his sophomore year began, the success of football still seemed more important to most students than scholarship. This disappointed Just. He was not getting the kind of intellectual stimulation that he had expected from discussions with other students. Lonely and discouraged, he was about ready to leave Dartmouth when he began his first science course—biology. In this course he read about one of the big mysteries of science, the development of the animal egg. This topic fascinated him, and biology became his true love as football had become so for so many other students. Just took every course in biology offered at Dartmouth. His work was outstanding. During his senior year he spent a good deal of his time on a research problem concerning the development and growth of the egg.

In June, 1907, Ernest Just graduated from Dartmouth with a degree in zoology. He was the only student in his class to graduate with highest honors. The deep interest that he had acquired in the development of the egg was to stay with him for the rest of his life.

Ernest Just went directly from Dartmouth to teach at Howard University in Washington, D.C., then and now, a predominantly black university. In 1912, he became head of the Department of Zoology at Howard, a position he held until his death in 1941. He was also on the faculty of Howard University's medical school as a professor and head of the Department of Physiology. His work toward improving medical education at Howard and at other medical schools for black students was extremely effective. His research studies into the nature of living cells began to attract the attention of many well-known biologists in the country.

Although as a scientist he was dedicated to teaching and working at Howard, Just left Washington each summer to carry on his research at the Marine Biological Laboratory at Woods Hole, on Cape Cod in Massachusetts. From 1909 to 1930, Just spent every summer except one in Woods Hole. The Marine Biological Laboratory is a very special place, famous in the history of biological science. It was here that Ernest Just carried out his greatest work in science.

THE MARINE BIOLOGICAL LABORATORY

At one time or another, practically all of the world's great biologists spend some time at the Marine Biological Laboratory in Woods Hole, Massachusetts. In the early 1900's, nearly every young scientist who was to make a name for himself would either study at the Laboratory or would study under people who had done so. Usually during the summer months, as they still do today, scientists and students would gather at MBL from colleges and universities in this country and abroad to study the varied and abundant marine animals available from the surrounding waters. In 1909, Dr. Frank R. Lillie from the University of Chicago was one such person. Ernest Just was to become one of his students, and later his collaborator and friend.

The Woods Hole Laboratory was also known as the place where students in the early stages of starting important research could be found during the summer. Some were destined to become great leaders like Just. Beginners in research always found special provisions for their laboratory needs at Woods Hole, and most of them came with their own professors. The discussions among students and professors have played an important part in careers begun and fostered at Woods Hole.

It is natural to wonder why a marine biological laboratory and the study of marine forms of life were important to biologists who were investigating basic problems of the life sciences. There are probably two reasons for this. First of all, the oceans have changed much less than the earth's surface throughout the history of the earth. Since the ocean environment has been so constant, there are reasons to believe that the first living things as we know them probably originated in the ocean waters. The oceans contain forms of animal life never found on the continents, and these forms represent every major group of animals in the animal kingdom especially adapted to the ocean environment. The rapid development of zoology and botany during the late 1800's naturally led to the establishment of marine research stations. Then, as more experimental methods began to be used in biology, it was found that marine specimens offered exceptional advantages for scientists investigating basic problems dealing with protoplasm, the living stuff inside cells. Sea water is very much like protoplasm. The fluids inside the bodies of most marine animals contain the same salts as the sea and in about the same proportions and concentrations. The eggs of many marine animals, such as sea urchins, starfish, and various worms are deposited in enormous numbers into sea water. When these eggs are taken into the laboratory for study and experimentation, they can be cultivated in glass dishes.

Ernest Just began his graduate studies at MBL in 1909 by taking a course in marine invertebrates (sea animals without backbones). During the summers of 1911 and 1912, he assisted Dr. Frank Lillie in fertilization studies and the breeding habits of the sandworm (Nereis) and the sea urchin (Arbacia). His work was so good that by 1916 he had completed six papers based on his work at MBL during the summer months.

Each spring after 1916, when his classes ended at Howard, Dr. Just headed north to Woods Hole to study with the world's leading scientists. The stimulating environment of alert, critical minds at Woods Hole did much toward developing Just as an outstanding scientist. He worked closely with Dr. Lillie, his first teacher at MBL, and they became good friends.

Dr. Just would usually arrive at Woods Hole three to four weeks before the other scientists and would leave after most had returned to their colleges at the summer's end. He would arrive early in order to work with the curator of the animal supply department and the animal collecting crew. Together they would carefully examine the marine animals to be used in his investigations during the summer months. Dr. Just insisted on having the best specimens possible to work with, and the collection methods affected the condition of the captured animals.

The eggs of marine animals, which were the center of Dr. Just's attention, lived for only about twenty-four hours outside a female animal's body. Dr. Just needed fresh eggs for much of his work. Sandworms hatched from eggs found in waters near the laboratory would swarm together only during the part of the month when the moon was between its third quarter phase and a full moon. Attracted by the light of the moon, they would appear swimming near the surface of the water about an hour after sunset. So at this time Dr. Just spent many evenings at the water's edge with a lantern, a net, and some glass collecting dishes. He would hold the lantern above the water and allow it to swing. The light from his lantern attracted the worms, which could readily be caught with a hand net. The males would appear first, shedding their sperm cells into the water. Masses of sperm cells looked like milky white clouds in the sea water. The females were attracted by the bright red color of the males as they whirled around the water surface in the area lit up by the lantern. The females would respond to the whirling motion of the males in the water by shedding their egg cells into the water. The worms shedding their reproductive cells were caught and placed in the same dishes. Then, or soon afterwards, the eggs would be fertilized by the sperm cells that have the ability to swim around in water. Since fertilized and unfertilized egg cells did not live long, Dr. Just had to make his observations at once. He would carry his dishes of worms and eggs back to his laboratory and work through the night studying the eggs under his microscope.

If Dr. Just wanted eggs and sperm to study the next day, then the male and female worms were kept in separate covered dishes overnight and placed in a sea-water table with water flowing over them. To obtain the eggs the following morning, he placed a female worm in clean sea water and snipped it with a sharp scissors. Eggs would pour forth quickly from the worm's body. The cut worm was removed immediately and the eggs were washed in clean sea water. The males were similarly washed in sea water and then dried with soft filter paper. Next they were cut in half between the head and tail. This provided Dr. Just with bloodless, dry sperm cells. The sperm were then mixed with a small amount of sea water; then two drops of this sperm suspension were added to the eggs of one female. The mixing of the sperm and egg cells was done under a microscope. This allowed Dr. Just to study every detail of the sperm entering the egg cell (fertilization) and the development of the egg that followed.

In the early 1900's some scientists had shown that the eggs of some marine animals could develop without being fertilized by a sperm. The name given to this phenomenon is *parthenogenesis.* If an egg was made to develop by something the scientist did to the egg in the laboratory, then it was known as *artificial parthenogenesis.* Full embryo development can be started in an egg (including frogs and rabbits) by a salt solution, electric shock, and a host of other artificial agents. This was shown by Jacques Loeb of the University of Chicago and T. H. Morgan of Columbia University in the first demonstration of artificial parthenogenesis at the turn of this century. In 1911, Dr. Frank Lillie, working at MBL in Woods Hole, allowed a sperm to become attached to the surface of an egg. He then pulled away the sperm so that it did not join the egg. This small contact between sperm and egg brought about some changes toward development inside the egg.

Jacques Loeb was considered to be a leader and well-known authority for his work in fertilization and especially artificial parthenogenesis. He founded a famous theory of fertilization, known as the lysin theory. This theory stated that *two* substances were needed for artificial parthenogenesis. First, according to Loeb, eggs must be treated with a chemical substance called butyric acid; then it must be treated with hypertonic sea water. (Hypertonic sea water has a higher concentration of salt than ordinary sea water.) Treatment with these two substances would cause eggs to develop into larvae that could swim in water. Furthermore, Loeb found that if the hypertonic sea water was used before the butyric acid the results would be the same. Loeb's theory lasted for about twenty years.

In 1922, Dr. Just made an attack on Loeb's famous theory. He presented evidence that the hypertonic sea water alone would start development of the egg of the sea urchin. During the summer of 1921 he produced free-swimming larvae of sea urchins by allowing only hypertonic sea water to act on unfertilized eggs of this marine animal. The larvae that he produced through artificial parthenogenesis looked no different from larvae developed from eggs that had been normally fertilized by sperm in the ocean. This sample of Just's work with the sea urchin egg shows how scientific theories must be questioned and altered when new evidence from experiments is produced. Just had shown that hypertonic sea water alone could do the job of parthenogenesis.

In addition to being a skillful experimenter and producer of knowledge, Dr. Just also had a great and rather playful imagination. He was not afraid to explore new fields and problems that others might think ridiculous. For example, he wondered if magnetism would affect the division of cells that followed egg fertilization. His few investigations into this area showed that magnetism did have some effect on cell division. It is interesting to note that in the late 1960's some space scientists were interested in the same question. In one of the biosatellites that carried a variety of animals and plants into outer space, sea urchin eggs were also sent along. Scientists wanted to study the effects, if any, of the Earth's magnetic field and radiation on the activity of these cells.

Dr. Just was a quiet man most of the time, especially while working at his laboratory bench. He would work for many hours without saying a single word to those working around him. He and Dr. Lillie used to carry on a game to see who would say the least number of words during the day while working in the lab together. One evening, at the supper table in the mess hall at MBL, Lillie remarked to those sitting around the table: "Well, I beat Just today. I said only three words." "Oh no," replied Just smiling. "I beat him today. I said only one."

EXPERIMENTS WITH
EGGS OF MARINE ANIMALS

Dr. Just came to know more about *normal* eggs and the *normal* egg development of marine life than any other investigator at Woods Hole. Other scientists would frequently seek him out for his advice on working with eggs. He would never do an experiment unless he was absolutely sure that his eggs were normal, for only normal ones would undergo normal development after fertilization. Dr. Just was often critical of the work of scientists whom he felt did not know what normal development was or who were using in experiments eggs that weren't normal to begin with. What was a normal egg to Dr. Just, and why was knowing about its development so important to him?

Dr. Just examined hundreds of eggs of different animals so that he would know and be able to recognize normal development of their eggs in the laboratory after fertilization. This was a laborious and long-enduring task. Once he knew what normal laboratory development was, then he could better recognize abnormal development if it occurred. Recognition of normal or abnormal egg development was important because of the kind of experiments that he carried out with eggs and fertilization. In his various experiments he would try to find out the effects of such things as temperature, salt concentration in sea water, ultraviolet light, magnetism, and evaporation of sea water on fertilization and subsequent egg development. These things might be called experimental factors. Before he set up or began an experiment, he would follow the development of the egg in the laboratory to be sure it was normal. Since a fertilized egg changes so quickly and dramatically during the first twenty-four hours, Dr. Just constantly had to watch the eggs through his microscope. If the egg or its development were not normal during the first hours after fertilization, then he could not be sure that any changes he later observed in the developing egg were caused by his experimental factor.

In order to start with normal eggs and have normal egg development in the laboratory, the laboratory conditions for the eggs must be exactly like the natural sea water conditions in the oceans. Over a period of years, Dr. Just learned from experience how to maintain natural conditions for eggs and how to handle them in the laboratory so they wouldn't be harmed in any way that would affect development before he used them. Because Dr. Just was so meticulous about starting with normal eggs, his experiments were highly productive and successful. In the 1800's and early 1900's much valuable time-saving research information had been lost because it passed from scientist to scientist by word of mouth. Just's fellow scientists urged him to make his knowledge of methods for successful experiments with marine eggs available to scientists at Woods Hole and others working in laboratories around the country. And so, in an attempt to preserve his knowledge of methods and techniques of working with marine eggs for the coming generation of scientists, Dr. Just wrote his first book. It was called, *Basic Methods for Experiments on Eggs of Marine Animals*. This book has been so important and useful over the years to scientists working in the United States and Europe that it was revised and updated in 1957 by scientists working at Woods Hole.

In this book Dr. Just described methods for handling in the laboratory the eggs and sperm cells of twenty-eight different kinds of marine animals. He included his techniques for preparing eggs on glass slides for viewing under a microscope. He also discussed such things as glassware, the use of sea water, and temperature which affected the nature of animals and eggs. To illustrate how careful his preparations for experimentation were, here are some of the things, learned from years of experience, which he said in his book.

On Cleanliness: The first rule to be observed by the experimenter in egg development is that of scrupulous cleanliness. Contamination in all forms must be avoided. It represents a serious source of error. *Be at great pains to insure the absolute cleanliness of every utensil used.* This precaution is as important as any taken against accidental contamination during the actual experimental work.

On Glassware: Ordinarily one uses an acid cleaner. After its use, the glassware should be washed in running water until the most delicate test for acid gives no reaction. Soap and soap powders, if not thoroughly removed, will modify experimental results when mixed with sea-water. I find that Bon Ami is superior to soap and soap powders because it is easily removed. It leaves the glassware bright and clear. After removing the dried Bon Ami with dry towels, the glassware is rinsed in running water for several minutes. *The glassware is then stacked upright, and never upside down for fear of chance contamination,* on dry linen towels. . . . I never use laboratory towels for drying glassware without having previously washed them in running water. . . .

On Temperature: It is well to record both the room temperature and that of sea-water containing eggs. One should have available two standardized thermometers. . . . The room temperature should be taken always in the same place in the room which should be protected against sunshine. The dishes containing the eggs, the temperature of which is taken, should be similarly placed and protected. In view of the fact that change in temperature is a very important experimental means, the worker should keep careful record of the temperature at which he conducts his experiments.... Further, unless eggs are normally found in sea-water of low temperature, *they should never be kept in the cold* except for the expressed purpose of investigating the effect of low temperature on an egg whose normal habitat is higher. I know of many investigators who have kept their animals on ice overnight in order to delay the shedding of eggs. This practice, I think can not be too severely condemned.

The Use of Sea-Water: Dishes containing eggs should always be protected against evaporation, because this makes the sea-water hypertonic and hypertonic sea-water is itself an experimental method. (Hypertonic sea-water is sea-water with a higher concentration of salt than usual.) More than once results have been reported as due to an experimental treatment which actually were brought about by the evaporation of the sea-water containing eggs. Therefore, the dishes should be covered. On warm days it is well to keep such dishes on the live table in running sea-water.... Dishes containing eggs should, of course, be protected against direct sunlight.

The Collection of Eggs: Many animals, especially those living at great depths of the sea, can not with profit be collected by the scientist himself. Here he must depend upon the collecting staff, the dredging apparatus and boats of the laboratory. However excellent the apparatus for the collecting may be, the factor of prime importance is the collectors. If these be inefficient or untrustworthy, the experimenter will suffer because of the bad condition of the animals furnished him.... Whenever the experimenter in egg development is dependent upon others for the collecting of breeding animals or of eggs, he must be confident that the collecting is properly accomplished. He should be sure that he has freshly collected organisms or cells; if these be aged, he has now to reckon with age as an additional complicating factor in his experiments. . . .

Dr. Just felt very strongly about these rules and others he set down about working with marine animals and their eggs. He looked unfavorably on scientists who didn't follow these simple rules but claimed results from their experiments. He even criticized them in his writing: "An experiment," he said, "should never in the least way be clouded by uncertainty concerning the normal process."

In the late 1920's, Dr. Frank Lillie, himself as authority on fertilization, and perhaps Just's closest colleague, said this about his former student:

In the twenty summer sessions that Just spent at the Marine Biological Laboratory at Woods Hole he became more widely acquainted with the embryological resources of the marine animals than probably any other person; and he learned to handle the material with skill and understanding. In consequence, he was in great demand, especially by physiologists who knew their physics and chemistry better than biology, for advice and assistance which he rendered generously. When he withdrew from Woods Hole to work in European laboratories, his loss to the scientific community was deeply felt.

DR. JUST GOES TO EUROPE

As a scientist, Dr. Ernest Just achieved and was respected. He was able, versatile, and productive. He was distinguished and recognized. He had received many awards and grants of money to support his research projects. He was a member of the corporation of the Marine Biological Laboratory and was on the editorial board of the *Biological Bulletin*, the official journal of MBL. His articles appeared in several European scientific journals as well as the *Biological Bulletin*. He was elected vice-president of American Society of Zoologists. However, as a man Dr. Just was frustrated and embittered. For even with his brains, insight, and great perseverance, he found the walls of racial prejudice and discrimination in America too high to climb. He felt, despite his ability and achievement, that he was not completely accepted at Woods Hole because he was a black man, and that there were limitations placed upon his career because of his race. He would not encourage other young black students to try for a career as a research biologist. Although he taught the biological sciences at Howard University during most of his life, he attempted to steer most of his students into careers as doctors rather than to follow in his footsteps. His students in pure biology from 1907 to 1941 were very few.

By 1930, Dr. Just still had much uncompleted work to do. He felt the need for greater opportunity for unlimited research facilities in foreign laboratories. Through no fault of its own, Howard University did not have the facilities to give full opportunity to his ambitions. This institution had cooperated fully over the years in granting him freedom and leaves of absence so that he could carry on his research at Woods Hole and elsewhere. To carry on his work he decided to leave Woods Hole and the United States, where the doors of the Rockefeller Institute for Medical Research had been closed to him because of prejudice and discrimination. In 1930, Dr. Just did not return to Woods Hole. He even gave up his teaching position at Howard which had meant so much to him during his lifetime. He was off to Europe to continue his research.

Dr. Frank Lillie perhaps knew Just better than most men did. In a tribute to his former student and collaborator, published in *Science* (January 2, 1942), shortly after Just's death, Dr. Lillie said:

> An element of tragedy ran through all Just's scientific career due to limitations imposed by being a Negro in America, to which he could make no lasting psychological adjustment in spite of earnest efforts on his part. The numerous grants for research did not compensate for failure to receive an appointment in one of the large universities or research institutes. He felt this as a social stigma, and hence unjust to a scientist of his recognized standing. In Europe he was received with universal kindness and made to feel at home in every way; he did not experience social discrimination on account of his race, and this contributed greatly to his happiness there. Hence, in part at least, his prolonged self-imposed exile on many occasions. That a man of his ability, scientific devotion, and of such strong personal loyalties as he gave and received, should have been warped in the land of his birth must remain a matter for regret.

Dr. Just appreciated Lillie's contribution to his development as a scientist. This was perhaps shown by the fact that during the summer of 1930, he cut short a study in Naples, Italy in order to return to Woods Hole. Many of the people that he had known and worked with during his years at MBL were surprised to see him. He showed up unannounced to participate in a special seminar in honor of Dr. Lillie's sixtieth birthday and fortieth anniversary as a worker at Woods Hole.

Dr. Just spent most of his last eleven years at famous European laboratories: in Germany at the Kaiser Wilhelm Institute for Biology in Berlin, in France at the Sorbonne and marine stations, and in Italy at the Naples Zoological Station. All of his appointments to these laboratories were limited in time. He never had the security of a life appointment adequate to carry out his work.

In November, 1938, in Paris, France, Dr. Just finished writing his second book, *The Biology of the Cell Surface*. In this book he brought together his life's work and thought on the fundamentals of living cells.

THE BIOLOGY OF THE CELL SURFACE

Dr. Just was a superb lecturer and an equally superb writer. The writing and publication of his second book while in Europe marked a fitting climax to his brilliant career as a scientist. For only two years later, in 1940, Dr. Just passed away in Washington, D.C.

In his book, Dr. Just summarized his numerous investigations. His investigations focused on only one type of a single living cell—the egg—and its development into a complex multicelled animal. From these he developed a general answer, or theory, about a very simple question: What is life? The answer to this question is really the ultimate goal of all biologists. Today, of course, scientists are still working to find better answers to it.

Dr. Just placed emphasis on the cell material lying around the outside edge of the cell and just inside the cell membrane. This region of the cell is called the ectoplasm of the cell. Most biologists up to Just's time had neglected the role of the ectoplasm and had centered on the nucleus of the cell as the "kernel of life." Just's attention to and definition of the ectoplasm was unique. He saw the ectoplasm as standing between the inner substance of the cell and the outside world. It reacts first to a stimulus outside the cell and conditions the behavior of the whole cell. Thus, by its location in the cell, the ectoplasm becomes important in the expression of life processes, according to Dr. Just. For example, some of Dr. Just's experiments had shown the role of ectoplasm in the intake and output of water from animal cells. Others of his experiments showed that in an egg without the ectoplasm, fertilization could not take place. And that in cell division after fertilization the ectoplasm has a lot to do with the formation of a new cell membrane.

Dr. Just's observations and deductions led him to emphasize the role of the ectoplasm. He was not saying that this region of the cell was the basis of life. Neither did he think that life rested in the nucleus or genes alone. Instead, he believed that life existed only when all cell parts and their activities were combined and worked together as a unit. His point about ectoplasm was that the individual role of the ectoplasm was a prime factor in cell development and growth. In his book he said: " . . . It (ectoplasm) is keyed to the outside world as no other part of the cell. It stands guard over the peculiar form of the living substance, is buffer against the attacks of the surroundings and the means of communication with it." Just regarded the surface of the cell as something more than a porous membrane.

There have not yet been any black Americans who have revolutionized man's thinking through science like an Einstein, Darwin, or Newton. To date, a Nobel prize has not been awarded to a black person for work in science. Dr. Just strove hard, not for prizes or world acclaim, but only to prove himself as a man in search of "the truth" through science, for the benefit of all people. In doing so, he perhaps has come the closest of any black American to revolutionizing our thinking about the nature of living substance.

MATTHEW A. HENSON

1865–1955

He Was First at the North Pole

Will you ever forget the date July 20, 1969? On that day two American astronauts first landed and walked on the moon. You probably sat in front of your television, awed and thrilled as you watched Neil Armstrong and Edwin Aldrin walk on the moon's surface. Trips to the moon are perhaps the most exciting and significant frontier in science today. If you had been a youngster in 1909, just 60 years before the first man on the moon, you would have been equally awed and thrilled by man's exploration of the Earth.

In the early 1900's some men were exploring the Earth's surface of ice and snow around the North Pole. At that time the feats of Arctic explorers were as dramatic as those of our astronauts. Expeditions to the cold, unknown ice-capped lands above Canada were as dangerous then as voyages to the moon or to the bottom of the sea are today.

An outstanding achievement in the investigation of the Earth's surface occurred on April 6, 1909. On that date two Americans discovered the Earth's geographic North Pole.

The first man to reach the North Pole was a black man. His name was Matthew Henson. About 45 minutes later Admiral Robert E. Peary, a Navy engineer and planner and commander of the polar expedition, joined Henson at the Pole. The temperature was 29° below zero. At the Pole the latitude is 90 degrees north, so every direction they stepped in was south. North, east, and west had vanished for Henson, Peary, and the four Eskimos who accompanied them to the Pole.

Get a globe of the Earth and find the North Pole. Take a quick look at the lands of ice and snow and the seas around the North Pole. Can you find Greenland? Imagine yourself surrounded by hundreds of miles of nothing but snow and floating glaciers. Use the scale on the globe to figure out how many miles your home is from the North Pole. The two American discoverers of the Pole left New York City in July 1908. How long did it take them to reach their goal?

Matthew Henson had been Peary's assistant on each of his explorations since 1888, the first being to Central America. Together, Peary and Henson had exposed themselves to the fierce stress of cold climate on six different trips to the Arctic's icelands. They showed what extreme cold a healthy human body could endure.

Reaching the Pole satisfied a dream that Peary and Henson had held for eighteen long years. The North Pole was the last major and most distant point for man to discover on Earth. Before Henson and Peary, others had tried for four centuries and failed—some losing their lives in the attempt.

An explorer is a special kind of scientist. He has the urge to know the unknown about some part of the universe. This urge is so strong that he risks his life to find out what lies on the other side of the ocean, at the bottom of the sea, or beyond the Earth's atmosphere. This urge pushed Marco Polo across Asia, Jacques Yves Cousteau beneath the sea, Armstrong and Aldrin to the moon, and Matthew Henson and Robert Peary to the North Pole.

In their role as scientists, explorers take their laboratories along with them. A ship can be one; so can a spacecraft, and the same thing applies to an outpost on the desert or at the North Pole. Today scientists live and work in laboratory stations in the Arctic and Antarctic regions. Some are studying polar weather. Others study long cylinder-shaped samplers of ice obtained by drilling into glaciers to depths of 7,000 feet or more.

Just as there were some similarities between the moon mission of our astronauts and those of the North Pole explorers, there were also differences. Henson and Peary hunted and fished for their food while on their expeditions. Little food provisions were taken along. Walrus were killed to feed the dogs that pulled their sleighs. The astronauts, on the other hand, take their food precooked and in neat packages. Their only problem is keeping weightless meals from floating around inside the spacecraft. Another interesting comparison has to do with how fast the news of the discoveries spread in 1909 and 1969. The world did not learn of the North Pole discovery until five months after the event. Yet when our astronauts stepped down on the moon, hundreds of millions of people the world over watched the actual event on television. It takes only 1.3 seconds for radio waves to travel between the moon and Earth.

Though more than sixty years separate Henson's achievement from that of our first moon astronauts, they shared the same dream of discovery and the quickening of the heartbeat that comes to explorers when they reach their goal. Before 1909, the North Pole was as remote as the surface of the moon seemed before Apollo 11. Henson and Peary filled in one of the last empty spaces on the globe in a quest for knowledge. The South Pole was discovered in 1912.

By training, Matthew Henson was not a scientist. Like many black boys and girls born in America in the 1800's, he was able to get little education. He never went to high school. He had no college degree. When Peary first asked Henson to accompany him on an expedition to Greenland, Henson replied, "I'd like to go, but what is there for me to do? I'm not a scientist." Little did he know what lay ahead, and the discoveries he would make for mankind.

GOING TO SCHOOL ON A SHIP

Matthew Henson had spent some adventurous years as a boy preparing for that famous day, April 6, 1909. He was born on a farm in Maryland a year after the end of the Civil War. His mother died when he was two, his father when he was eight. At 11, to escape an unhappy life with a cruel stepmother, he ran away to Washington to find an uncle he had never met.

The young boy found his uncle and lived with him for several years. His uncle sent him to school, but he left to work as a dishwasher in a small restaurant when his uncle could no longer care for him. Working at the restaurant, he heard customers talk about the docks at Baltimore and the large ships that sailed all over the world from there. This talk gave him an urge to see the world, and find adventure in becoming a sailor.

At 13 he quit his dishwashing job and hiked to Baltimore. Here he signed on as a cabin boy on a ship bound for Hong Kong. The voyage to China took many months. The captain of the sailing vessel began to teach young Henson how to read and write. Each day the captain's cabin became a classroom for his cabin boy. The captain also taught him seamanship, navigation, geography, mathematics. Matt learned from experience how to apply first-aid to sailors injured aboard the ship.

Matt Henson lived on the oceans for five years. These were important years in his life, but little did he realize it at the time. He became an able-bodied seaman, sailing to China, Japan, Manila, North Africa, Spain, France, and through the Black Sea to southern Russia.

Henson's travels introduced him to many languages. Some he learned well. He also learned how peoples of different lands lived, and how to live with them. One winter his ship was ice-locked in a Russian harbor. During this winter stopover he learned to speak Russian, hunt wolves, and drive sleighs through the snow.

When the captain of his ship, his first and only real teacher, died at sea, Henson left the ship that had been his home for five years. At 17 he went to Newfoundland on a fishing boat and then on to Boston, Providence, Buffalo, and New York, working at various odd jobs. At nineteen he returned to Washington and took a job as a stockboy in a men's clothing store. This job changed his whole life, and the history of world exploration.

HENSON MEETS PEARY

In 1888, Robert E. Peary was a civil engineer for the U.S. Navy. He had made a trip to Nicaragua in Central America to lay out the route for a ship canal between the Atlantic and Pacific Ocean. In 1886, searching for adventure, he shipped toward the Arctic on a whaling ship, getting off in Greenland. He spent several months surveying Greenland's icy coast.

This first Greenland experience made him anxious for another trip north. He wanted to be the first man to cross Greenland on foot. Back in Washinton he could find no support for this venture from government scientists or the public. The following year he found himself assigned again to the Nicaragua Ship Canal project. His ideas about returning to Greenland had to be put aside. In preparation for his return to Nicaragua, he went to a store that sold clothes suitable for the warm tropical climates of Central America. He needed a tropical sun helmet.

Matt Henson was in the back room of the store taking a stock inventory when Peary entered. The store owner called back to Matt to bring out a size seven and three-eighths sun helmet. The store owner knew Peary well and had told him earlier about the excellent work of his stockboy.

When Matt came out with the helmet, Peary introduced himself. He then tried on the helmet, bought it, and began talking to his new acquaintance. Peary told Matt about the canal survey job to be finished in Nicaragua and asked him if he wanted to go along with him as his servant. Henson accepted this opportunity to travel again.

The canal survey party spent seven months in Nicaragua. During this time Matt Henson showed that he had many skills and much ingenuity. Peary made him a field assistant to the surveying crew. This was the beginning of a twenty-three-year association in which Henson and Peary worked and traveled together.

While in Nicaragua Henson learned of Peary's burning desire to cross Greenland and someday to discover the North Pole. Upon returning from Central America, Peary asked Henson to go to Greenland with him to explore the ice-bound wilderness. Peary had no financial backing for his second expedition; Henson agreed, however, to go without pay whenever Peary was ready.

To Matthew Henson this was more than an opportunity for adventure, which he loved; he also wanted to prove that he was as brave, intelligent, and strong as a white man. Matthew Henson went to the frozen lands of the Arctic six times with Peary, in the years 1891, 1893, 1898, 1905, and 1908.

1891–1892

In June, 1891, Henson started on his first trip to the Arctic region with Peary. The purpose of this expedition was to cross the northern region of Greenland from the west to east coast. Seven people, including Peary and Henson, left on a ship from New York. They included a doctor, a bird watcher, a geologist, a skier out for adventure, and Peary's wife. They carried with them food—tea biscuits, pea soup, dried beef, and fruit—cooking equipment, tents, sleeping bags, and scientific equipment—photographic supplies, thermometers, compasses, a barometer, and a pocket sextant.

In late July, Peary's ship left his party on the rocky shore of McCormick Bay in Greenland. The ship was to return for them a year later. The fall and winter were spent making preparations for the march across Greenland in the spring.

Henson set to work building a wooden house that would serve as headquarters. He built sleighs to be pulled by dogs over the ice and snow. The dogs were obtained from the Eskimos who traded them for guns and ammunition.

When the winter storms let up, Peary and the skier set out to cross the Greenland ice cap. Everyone wanted to go, but Peary decided that a small team could travel faster than a larger one and less food would have to be carried. So Henson and the others remained behind. He spent most of his days with the Eskimos.

Henson became a close companion to the Eskimos he met. He learned to speak their language, dress in their clothes, live in their homes, and eat their food. Hunting, trapping, and fishing on the frozen lands and water were some of the things he learned to do well. He knew that if he was to survive in this strange land of bitter cold he would have to learn from the natives. The knowledge and skills that he acquired were used to help all of the people in his party. Peary depended heavily on Henson's skills, knowledge, and work.

When July passed, Peary and his traveling companion had not returned to headquarters. The waiting party became worried. Henson pictured Peary falling into a crevice in a glacier and his body lying buried in the snow. During the first week in August the ship returned to carry the party home. Still no Peary. Henson readied a rescue team. But before he could set out in search, Peary and his sportsman companion returned. They had been triumphant, returning from a round trip of about 1200 miles, exhausted, weakened from exposure to the frigid climate, and near starvation.

Back in the United States, Peary began making plans for another trip to the Arctic. He and Henson went on a lecture tour around the country telling about their Greenland expedition. Reaching the North Pole was now foremost in their minds.

The North Pole was just a pinpoint, but it was the region around the Pole that was important. Man and science would not be satisfied until man came within a few miles of the Pole. No one knew how it was to be reached. Could it be by way of Greenland? What lay beyond the drifting floes of Polar Sea ice?

1893–1897

In June, 1893, Henson, Peary, Peary's wife, and eight others steamed north again. A large crowd cheered the party as they pulled away from a dock in New York City. Newspapers carried enthusiastic stories about this expedition. Peary planned to go further north than he had on his last trip.

Arriving in Greenland on August 3, the party began preparations for the coming winter and spring. A house was built near the shore of Bowdoin Bay. Henson built sleighs to carry supplies. During the fall, trips were made far inland to leave supplies along the ice cap trail that was to be traveled during the spring march. The supplies were marked by ten-foot wooden poles driven into the hard snow.

Weather conditions were severe. The party leaving supplies was turned back by raging snow storms. A huge piece of glacier falling into the bay smashed small boats holding barrels of fuel oil for the winter months. Many barrels were lost in the icy waters of the bay. By the time winter set in the advance supplies had not been set up on the inland ice. Without these food and fuel supplies, chances of reaching the Pole in the spring were not good.

Nevertheless, in March, 1894, Peary set out for the interior of Greenland. At one point, 125 miles from home base, the temperature dipped 40 degrees below zero. Fierce winds and blinding snow made traveling practically impossible. Forty-eight-mile-per-hour winds and the extremely low temperatures were more than the sleigh dogs could stand. Many froze to death. Several members of the party were crippled by frostbite, and Peary was forced to return to headquarters. It took six weeks for his weakened men to recuperate from the exhaustion and frostbite.

This first year had brought many hardships and disappointments. All but three members of the original party decided to return to the United States in August of 1894. Henson, Peary, and Lee, a reporter, remained to spend another winter. During the winter of 1894-1895 they discovered three big meteorites that they had heard the Eskimos talk about as "stones from heaven."

Peary and Henson had learned something important from their first year of defeat. The field party, to reach the Pole, would have to be small. During April, 1895, Peary, Henson, and Lee crossed the 450 miles of the ice cap of North Greenland with three sleighs and 37 dogs. They wanted to map the northeastern region of Greenland. Peary wanted to know whether Greenland extended to the North Pole, or whether there was a frozen sea between Greenland and the Pole. The rugged condition of the country made exploration difficult. Food supplies ran low. On June 25, the three men arrived back at home base with only one sleigh and one dog. Some of the dogs had been killed and used as food by the men. Lee, sick and crippled by the cold, was pulled into home base on a sleigh pulled by Peary, Henson, and the one remaining dog. This expedition had been a long struggle to stay alive.

Peary and Henson gained an important bit of knowledge from this trip. Greenland was certainly an island. A sea of ice floes lay between it and the Pole. They knew the next expedition would have to be long—maybe three or four years.

In August, their ship returned to carry them home. With them they carried two of the three meteorites discovered during the past winter. The third was too heavy to manage aboard the ship. Their scientific prizes also included walrus hides and other animal specimens captured by Henson. Henson busied himself skinning the walrus hides during the voyage back to New York.

The two meteorites were placed on display at the American Museum of Natural history in New York, where you can see them today. Henson went to work in the taxidermy department of the Museum of Natural History. He had become an authority in his knowledge of the Arctic, its weather, landscape, and animal life. At the museum he was responsible for mounting the walrus skins and arranging true-to-nature exhibits of the beasts and backgrounds of the far North. He helped to plan exhibits of Eskimo villages, showing their skin tents and snow igloos used while out on hunting trips. Henson worked at the museum for two years.

In the summer of 1897, he returned with Peary to bring home the third meteorite. It weighed seventy tons and was the largest meteorite known at the time. Today it too can be found at the Museum of Natural History in New York. On their voyage back with the huge meteorite, Peary and Henson talked about their determination to reach the Pole. After returning with the third and largest meteorite, Henson returned to his museum work and Peary went to London. Here he received a medal from the Royal Geographical Society and a ship for his next polar expedition.

Henson was still working at the museum when Peary called him in the spring of 1898. Henson had done extremely well there and he enjoyed his work. He was thinking of marriage and settling down in a home for the first time in his life. Peary asked Henson once again to leave with him in July for a Polar attempt. He was planning to take along only Henson and a doctor. This was his preference despite objection from some of his supporters about his taking a black man with him. Some thought Henson should be replaced by a white man.

1898–1902 FOUR LOST YEARS

In the summer of 1898, Peary and Henson were headed north again, a doctor accompanying them. They were hoping to make the Pole this time. The next four years were spent in regions above north Greenland. They were disastrous years.

Peary had planned to push his ship into the Arctic Ocean and use it as a base from which to travel to the Pole. But the ship became locked in ice for the winter short of the Arctic Ocean. This was the first serious setback. They had to carry supplies overland to set up headquarters at Fort Conger. Fortunately, housing had been built and was intact at Conger, having been left by a previous group of Arctic explorers. Fort Conger was 400 miles from the North Pole. The ice of the Arctic Ocean lay between Fort Conger and the Pole.

While crossing the ice cap to Fort Conger in January 1899, Peary's feet froze, and his toes were severly frostbitten. The pain in his feet put Peary in agony. Gangrene set in and the doctor had to remove seven of his toes. Henson cared for Peary during the painful ordeal of waiting for the stumps of his toes to heal. All attempts to reach the Pole that season were abandoned.

By March, 1900, Peary had recovered and he and Henson made another drive northward. Only one Eskimo would dare go with them. Peary's crippled feet made the march slow and troublesome over the sea ice. Again they were forced to turn back.

In the spring of 1902, they tried again. Supplies and food gave out. Their sleighs collapsed. For the third time they had to turn back to home base.

In 1902, Peary, Henson, and seven Eskimos made another try. They ran into storm after storm of blinding snow. On April 21, they were 343 miles from the Pole. The Eskimos feared the storm and turned back. The dogs broke down under the strain. Food supplies reached low levels again. Peary and Henson were forced to turn around a fourth time and head south. They returned dejected to New York in August of 1902.

Although Peary and Henson were discouraged, they had been able to make maps of regions largely unknown to man. They had found that the route to the Pole by the northwest coast of Greenland was impossible, and they had learned some techniques of traveling over sea ice.

During the next three years Peary made plans to attack the Pole again. He had a ship built with engines powerful enough to smash through the ice-clogged seas. Henson took a job on the railroad and traveled throughout the United States.

1905–1906 CLOSE TO THE POLE

In July, 1905, Peary's newly built ship was ready. Peary, Henson, a doctor, and a weather expert were northward-bound again. By September their ship reached a latitude of 82°27′ north. This was the farthest north any vessel had ever penetrated the icy Arctic waters.

At the edge of the Arctic Ocean they settled down to prepare for the intended spring expedition to the Pole, which was about 500 miles away. In early spring they began the march across the iced ocean with 22 Eskimos, 20 sleighs, and 131 dogs. Henson took the lead to leave supplies and find the best trails for others to follow. The ice peaks began to melt and break apart early; this made the going treacherous. Many times they stood at the edge of an ice pack facing open water. The march couldn't continue on until the water froze over. Furious storms forced delays and loss of traveling days. They succeeded, however, in reaching a point 87°6′ north latitude, break-ing a record for Polar expeditions. They were 125 miles from their goal. No man had ever gone so far north. Hardships, hunger, and cold forced them to turn back.

The return journey was a hardship too. Two blades were broken off the ship's propeller, and the rudder was damaged from smashing into an ice pack. Water had poured into the ship through a hole made when the stern hit a point of ice. On Christmas Eve, 1906, the ex-pedition entered New York harbor, on its battered ship.

This was to have been Peary's last attempt to reach the Pole. However, within days after arriving home he had announced his intention to return for another try. In March, 1907, the Peary Arctic Club decided to support Peary for one more try, whereupon Peary immediately arranged to have his ship repaired.

The repairs were to have readied the ship to sail that summer but work schedules fell behind. The postponement gave Henson time to get married. After his honeymoon he returned to take charge of the ship's repairs.

OFF FOR THE POLE

On July 6, 1908, the ship was ready to steam out of New York for the north again. Henson had waited a year and a half for this day. He had been married about a year, and leaving his wife was difficult. He hoped that the next time she saw him it would be with feelings of joy and happiness, and that she would be glad she had permitted him to leave her, knowing that he might not return.

Peary took five men with him in addition to Henson. There was the ship's master, Captain Bartlett; a surgeon, Dr. J. W. Goodsell; a secretary, Ross Marvin; and two young explorers, George Borup and Donald MacMillan.

The ship had been named in honor of President Theodore Roosevelt. On July 7, the Roosevelt stopped at Oyster Bay, in Long Island Sound. President Roosevelt came aboard to add his words of encouragement to Peary and his party. They were off! The ship headed straight for Greenland.

By August 12, Etah Harbor on the west coast of Greenland was reached. The trip so far was uneventful.

They went ashore to trade with the Eskimos, offering them clothing in exchange for whale and walrus meat, dogs, and skins. Henson was so busy on board he couldn't keep his diary up to date. Peary was constantly saying, "Matt do this," and "Matt do that." The Eskimos were a big problem, because so many wanted to come aboard and stay. Forty-nine Eskimo men, women, and children were kept. They were good workers, even the children.

It took 21 days to go further north from Etah to Cape Sheridan, fighting almost impassable ice. Henson worked on the sleighs to be used that winter. The Eskimo women made the clothing for the men to wear during the winter. Small life boats were packed with food and supplies in case the Roosevelt was lost.

At Cape Sheridan, Henson continued working on the sleighs, which were to be different from those used on the earlier expeditions. Fresh meat was a necessity, and hunting musk-oxen and reindeer for this purpose took many hours. Also the dark winter days were quickly approaching, and their preparations had to be well advanced while there was still light.

All winter long small parties were moving provisions and equipment to Cape Columbia, the next advance base, 93 miles to the northwest. The trail from the ship at Cape Sheridan to Cape Columbia was kept open all winter by the constant travel between the two points. Loads of supplies were left at Cape Columbia. There were frequent storms and intense cold. Henson saw rocks weighing at least 100 pounds picked up and blown by the wind during snow storms to distances of more than 100 feet.

Henson, his dogs, and a sleigh packed with supplies

On February 18, Henson and a small group of Eskimos left the Roosevelt at Sheridan for the long march to the Pole. The ship's captain and doctor had already gone ahead to Cape Columbia. Falling snow, loose and deep on the ground, heavy winds, and intense cold made the

are ready for a trip across the frozen arctic snows.

going slow. Loads on each sleigh weighed about 500 pounds. They slept in igloos at night. Even the Eskimos suffered from the cold, and some turned back. The frozen big toe of one Eskimo was thawed by placing it under Henson's bearskin shirt and against the heat of his body. Bubbles in their thermometers made them unusable. When the brandy began to freeze, they realized it was at least 45° below zero. On February 22, Cape Columbia was reached.

Peary and the remainder of his party had not left the Roosevelt at Sheridan until February 21. While waiting at Cape Columbia for his arrival, the sleighs loads were readjusted. Gale winds had destroyed the igloo built earlier during the winter, so a new one was constructed. The scene was bleak and desolate. Peary arrived with his team on February 26.

From Cape Columbia, Henson and Peary were to leave the land and cross over an ice-covered ocean, 430 miles north, to find the Pole.

HENSON SHOWED THE WAY

Peary wasted no time. Preparations were made carefully. Assignments were given to each member of the party and the 24 Eskimos. There were six teams. Each man had his dogs, sleighs, and Eskimos to command.

Captain Bartlett and Borup left separately with their teams of Eskimos on February 26 to lay down the northward trail and build igloos along the way. Bartlett was first off. Borup returned after three days to start out again with a new load of supplies.

At 6:30 a.m. on March 1, Henson and his three Eskimos took the lead following the trail laid by Bartlett. Marvin, MacMillan, and Peary broke camp later on.

After traveling a quarter of a mile on foot at the outset, each team left the land ice and moved onto sea ice. The sea ice was much rougher. Pickaxes were needed to forge their steps ahead. Sleighs broke easily on the rough trail and had to be repaired in sub-zero temperatures. Strong gale winds blew continuously. The extreme cold numbed their cheeks and noses.

While one team slept, another was able to catch up with it. The first team then moved on while the team behind slept. This system of marches went on for 14 days.

On March 14, Peary sent his first support party back to Camp Columbia on land. Dr. Goodsell, MacMillan, and four Eskimos made up this first returning party. Temperatures had been 49° to 59° below zero, and MacMillan had a frozen heel.

Peary's general plan was to continue like this. At the end of a certain number of days certain parties would turn back to the land and the ship. By the end of March all had returned except Bartlett, Peary, Henson, and seven Eskimos. On April 1, Bartlett and his Eskimo team went the farthest north that anyone had ever been. He went to 87°47′ north latitude to blaze the trail for those who would make the forward march to the Pole. While waiting for Bartlett and his team to return, Peary, Henson, and four Eskimos picked out the strongest dogs and rearranged the supplies on the sleighs. Then, awaiting Bartlett's return, they were able to get some 30 hours of rest.

Bartlett returned and described with pride his march to the farthest point north. He told Peary what to expect up to 87°47′ north latitude. Bartlett and his Eskimo aids then bid Peary and Henson goodbye. As Bartlett journeyed back to land, Henson and Peary headed for the Pole. They planned five quick daily marches of 25 miles a day. Peary was in fairly good condition. Up to this point he had brought up the rear and had used the trails made by his support parties.

APRIL 6, 1909—THE POLE!

The sun was constantly on their backs in a never-ending day. A southeast wind was pushing them on. Each day Peary and Henson became more tired and worn. Their bodies ached. Shifting ice was dangerous. When they reached Bartlett's farthest point north, they were 133 miles from the Pole.

On April 4, they were 60 miles from the Pole. Henson moved ahead as the trail-blazer. Peary and the four Eskimos followed. On April 5, Peary made an observation with his instruments, and found that they were about 35 miles from the Pole.

No sextant was accurate enough to show the exact pinpoint that was the North Pole. Just how close a man had to be to the Pole to claim he had reached it was a matter of opinion. Most scientists felt that if a person came within 10 to 20 miles of the Pole, this would be close enough to claim the Pole. The North Pole is a needlepoint in the middle of a huge mass of shifting ice. The exact point may be atop an iceberg one day, a spot on the surface of a pool of water on another day, and a point on a ridge of snow on another.

The night of April 5, 1909, was sleepless for Henson and Peary; only the Eskimos slept well. Henson and Peary were too excited to sleep. The Eskimos ignorant of the Earth's shape and geography, scarcely realized that Peary and Henson were about to make a great discovery—that history was to be made within hours.

On April 6, Henson was the first to break camp. Peary followed more slowly with three of the Eskimos. The long daily marches and the lack of rest had drained his body of energy. At one point he was an hour behind Henson. He was able to keep up only by covering most of the distance riding in one of the sleighs. At about 10:00 a.m., Henson stopped his march, as he felt he had covered enough miles to have reached the Pole. He and his one Eskimo aid began to build an igloo. Henson thought they were close enough. Peary with three Eskimos caught up to Henson 45 minutes later. He unpacked his observational equipment; he took careful measurements of the sun's altitude. His calculations placed him at $89°57'$. Ninety degrees north would be the true top. This was it. They were within the region considered by scientists to be the North Pole. They knew it was impossible to exactly locate $90°$ north with the instruments they had.

Later in the day, after three hours' sleep, Henson and Peary moved several miles beyond this first measured latitude. Peary took another observation and found himself south of the North Pole. They turned around and returned back to the igloo for a night's rest. Their only direction was south.

The next morning, April 7, more observations of the sun were made. Photographs were taken of the icy terrain. Weather observations were written down. With a sounding instrument they recorded the depth of the Polar Sea to be greater than 9,000 feet at the point where they were. While Peary made many measurements, Henson recorded the figures as Peary called them out. Late in the day Peary made sure that he photographed

Henson and the four Eskimos holding flags. Henson held the American flag.

WHY HENSON WENT TO THE POLE

Henson risked his life, as did Peary, to claim the Pole for the United States. Upon their return home, Henson lectured about their discovery while Peary wrote a scientific report to prove they had reached the Pole. His report was sent to the National Geographic Society. After his lecture tour, Henson wrote a book about his adventure with Peary: *A Negro at the North Pole.*

Why did Peary select a black man to go with him to the Pole rather than one of his white assistants? This might seem like a ridiculous question to ask, but it was asked many times after Peary, Henson, and other members of the support party had returned to the United States. Some people even criticized Peary for taking Henson rather than Captain Bartlett.

Undoubtedly, most of the critics lacked a real understanding of the problems of Polar work and travel. Few people knew what it meant to travel over the rough ice of the Polar Sea. Most were ignorant of the entire history of Polar exploration and what Henson and Peary had gone through and learned together for over 20 years. There was no understanding of how sleighs had to be built for the rough conditions of travel in Greenland, how food and fuel had to be carried, and how to drive the dogs to pull the sleighs. Feeding the dogs and keeping them healthy was an art in itself. Also, how to dress to withstand the bitter temperatures of 60° and 70° below zero was something new to be learned for men used to a far warmer climate. All this essential knowledge could only be acquired in actual work. There was no opportunity to practice as today's astronauts do, in laboratories, before their big missions into outer space. Lack of understanding of the skills required of a man to reach the Pole was perhaps the main reason why people criticized Peary for taking Henson with him. They did not realize that Henson was the only man who had mastered all the skills.

Matthew Henson first went north with Peary in 1891. He accompanied Peary in 1893 over the Greenland ice-cap. Together they rounded the northern end of Greenland in 1900. He shared with Peary the four heartbreak years from 1898 to 1902. He helped Peary break the record for going the farthest north, in 1906. Henson always got along well with the Eskimos; he could talk their language, and the Eskimos' assistance was essential to Peary's mission. Henson built the sleighs and repaired them. Several times he saved Peary's life.

During the winter of 1909, while still on board the Roosevelt, Peary told Macmillan about his plans for the Polar attempt to be made in the spring. He told Mac-Millan that after each man had worked up to a certain point they would return to home base. Peary felt that support parties would no longer be needed once he got close to the Pole. But, said Peary to MacMillan, "Henson is not to return; I can't get along without him."

And so, Matthew Henson became a co-discoverer of the North Pole. He had been indispensable in this great discovery. He belongs to that small group of searchers who have given us knowledge about our world and our universe.

GEORGE WASHINGTON CARVER

1864–1943

He Studied Peanuts

Butter	Wood filler	Oil
Soap	Meat sauce	Linoleum
Breakfast cereal	Leather dyes	Shaving cream
Face cream	Bleach	Paper
Dried coffee	Plastics	Ink
Wood stain	Synthetic rubber	Metal polish
		Candy

Do these products seem related in any way?

In January, 1921, a black man stood before the Ways and Means Committee of the United States House of Representatives in Washington D.C. From a cardboard suitcase he pulled out bags, tubes, and bottles containing the products above, and more. Some thirty small bottles held dyes made from peanut skins. Another bottle held a creamy peanut butter. Another held face cream made with a peanut oil base. The bags contained food for cattle, instant dried coffee, and breakfast cereal. There was ice cream powder to be mixed with water and frozen like ice cream made from dairy cream. And there was milk too, made from peanuts. This special milk had been given to starving babies in Africa, where animal milk was lacking.

The black man was George Washington Carver. He was a plant scientist. "Gentlemen," he said, "I have been studying the peanut. All of these products before you were made with substances taken from peanuts. They were developed in my research laboratory at Tuskegee Institute in Tuskegee, Alabama."

Mr. Carver had come to Washington at the request of the United Peanut Growers Association. The Congressmen were considering a tariff bill that was to give protection to America's crop farmers. The Association wanted peanuts included in the tariff bill. Rice, peanuts, and other food crops grown in China and Japan could sell for less money in the United States. This was unwanted competition for Southern farmers. A tax on imported food crops would make the prices of these foods equal to those crops grown in the United States.

For two days the Congressional committee had listened to people talk about rice, wheat, and tobacco protection. Scientist Carver was the last to be heard. Listening to a black man talk about the possibilities of peanuts was the last thing they expected to hear. After all, the peanut plant had been considered a worthless weed. Peanuts were monkey food—something to chew on at the circus or baseball game. Some Congressmen thought Carver and his peanuts were just a joke to end the three long days of hearings.

Mr. Carver was to have talked for only ten minutes. But he captured the attention of the Congressmen and was allowed to talk on and answer many questions. He spoke of sweet potatoes and exhibited some of the products created from this crop—ink, pomade, mucilage, relishes, and flour. He held up a bottle of syrup made from sweet potatoes that could be used to hold peanuts together in a peanut candy bar.

But the scientist from Tuskegee went back to his peanuts. He claimed they had more possibilities than sweet potatoes. He explained how the peanut was one of the richest products of the soil. It was rich in food value and other chemical substances that could be used in various industries. The peanut, he said, could keep hungry people healthy and make Southern farmers wealthy.

"I have even made artificial meat dishes from pea-nuts. As science develops the products of nature, we are going to use less and less meat," Carver went on. (It is interesting to know that today, some meat companies in the United States have produced artificial meat using plant fibers from soybeans. You can buy this "woven" meat in some supermarkets.)

At the end of this last day of testimony, Mr. Carver walked down the steps of the United States Capitol build-ing alone with his heavy suitcase in hand. He headed back to his small laboratory at Tuskegee. In a later meeting the Congressional committee voted to include the peanut in the new tariff bill. Peanuts were no longer "peanuts."

FROM PAINTER TO PLANT SCIENTIST

George Washington Carver was an extraordinary man. His life before coming to Tuskegee in 1896 had been extraordinary too—difficult and sometimes cruel. As a young boy he had been raised by a white farmer and his wife, the Carvers, in Diamond Grove, Missouri. George's mother, a slave woman who worked for the Carvers, was kidnapped from the Carver farm by slave raiders before George was a year old. His father, a slave on a farm near the Carvers, was accidentally killed before his mother disappeared. George and his older brother never knew their own parents. Farmer Carver gave them his name.

George grew up lonely, sickly, but with a very curious and intelligent mind. He wanted to know everything there was to know about plants and animals. However, he had no science books and there were no nearby schools for black children. So George had plenty of time to roam the woods and fields around the Carver farm. He learned much by studying nature in the wild. Plants became his toys and animals his playmates. He picked flowers, grasses, and fruits and collected frogs, grasshoppers, and tree barks. He would ask himself simple questions. Why is grass green? What are flowers for? How does a seed make a plant? Why do plants die?

When George found plants that were wilting or dying, he would dig them up, bring them home, and nurse them back to health. He did this alone and quietly in his secret garden. During cold winter months George protected his plants from the cold by caring for them inside a barn. Neighborhood friends of the Carvers called him "the Plant Doctor."

George was in love with nature. He believed that God would tell him everything he wanted to know about plants if he carefully and patiently cared for them. He was a keen observer, able to see more in plants and flowers than others could. This ability was later to appear in his very detailed paintings and drawings of plants.

At ten years of age, George struck out on his own to get an education. He wandered in poverty about the countryside of Missouri and Kansas, attending school and working as a farmhand, cook, and laundry helper. In Minneapolis, Kansas, he settled down to attend and graduate from high school. At every chance, he worked among plants and flowers. But, not being able to have his own permanent garden, he began to draw and paint. The lifelike details of his paintings showed how much he observed and knew about plants.

At twenty-five years of age George Carver gained admission to Simpson College in Iowa. In his first attempt to attend a college in Kansas, he was rejected because he was black. He continued his painting at Simpson, and his desire to study botany grew stronger. Despite his ability as a painter, George's art teacher felt that he could never make a living from art, especially since he was black. When she learned of his strong interest in botany from his paintings and his good work in science courses, she wrote to her father, a professor of horticulture at Iowa State College.

So, after two years at Simpson College, George was admitted to study in the agricultural department at Iowa State College. He worked in the greenhouse and laboratory to earn his living money and tuition. When he wasn't working he was studying botany, chemistry, geometry, bacteriology, zoology, and entomology. He continued his painting too. His love for plants and skill in painting helped him to win several prizes for still-life pictures at the Iowa Exhibit of State Artists. One of his paintings was sent to the World's Fair at Chicago, where it won an honorable mention award.

In 1894, George Carver graduated from Iowa State College with high honors. Agriculture was becoming more of a science. He remained at Iowa to study for another degree. Because of his outstanding work with plants and soils, he was made an assistant instructor in botany and was appointed director of the greenhouse. His passion for plants deepened. In cross-fertilization, the propagation of plants, and the study of plant diseases, he did outstanding work. In 1896, he received his master's degree in agriculture and botany. His work in agricultural science was becoming widely known. Other scientists began to look to George Washington Carver as an authority. In 1897, he reported for the first time in America a new kind of taphrina, a fungus plant that grows on the leaves of red and silver maple trees. In later years, this species of fungus was given the scientific name of taphrina Carveri after its discoverer.

THE CALL FROM TUSKEGEE

In 1881, Booker T. Washington, a black educator, became the first president of a new school for blacks in Tuskegee, Alabama. One of the most important things that Booker T. Washington ever did was to ask George Washington Carver to become head of the Department of Agriculture at Tuskegee Institute in 1896. This would involve directing agricultural research and teaching natural science to Southern farmers, who at that time urgently needed help. In order to support a large number of poor people, they needed to learn how to use the soil and also how to grow and harvest a variety of crops.

George Washington Carver accepted the invitation from Booker T. Washington to join the faculty at Tuskegee Institute. It was there that he eventually became famous and in turn helped make Tuskegee Institute as famous as it is today.

When he arrived at the school there was little for him to work on and nothing to work with. Washington wanted an agricultural laboratory. But there was little equipment and even less money to buy any. Washington's new teacher-scientist, being quiet and shy, liked to work alone, and so he asked for a room of his own for a laboratory. Today, in the George Washington Carver Museum, you can see the crude laboratory equipment that Carver made for his first laboratory. Carver's philosophy was to start with what you have and make something of it. For heat he adapted an old barn lantern. A heavy kitchen cup became his mortar, a vessel in which to grind up substances. A flat piece of iron was used to pulverize substances placed in his mortar. He made beakers by cutting off the tops of old bottles found at the dump. An ink bottle was turned into an alcohol lamp. From plant fibers, Carver made a wick for his lamp.

From Carver's small laboratory at Tuskegee came the discoveries and products that enriched the Southern farmer, the whole of America, and eventually, the world. During Carver's first year at Tuskegee, Mr. Washington persuaded the Alabama State Legislature to finance the Tuskegee Agricultural Experiment Station. Carver was made director of the station. He began to demonstrate how science could be used by showing farmers new ways of fertilizing soil and planting seeds.

FROM COTTON TO PEANUTS

The things learned from Carver's experiments at the Experiment Station were used to help Southern farmers—black and white—to prosperity. He helped them in several important ways, such as making more medicines from plants, detecting and fighting plant diseases, conservation and fertilization of the soil and the raising of healthier livestock. Farmers traveled many miles and from distant states to listen to Carver. One of his greatest accomplishments was in persuading the farmer to grow crops other than cotton.

Cotton had been raised in the South for over one hundred years. Easy to grow but difficult to harvest, it was the basis of the South's economy. The cotton was shipped to England and spun into cloth. Before the Civil War, slaves in America were used to build the cotton industry and keep it expanding. Slaves planted, picked, and cleaned the cotton by hand.

After the Civil War, which ended legal slavery, cotton continued to be the main farm industry. Ex-slaves who became tenant farmers, and the white plantation owners for whom they worked, continued to depend on cotton for a living. Most blacks still lived and worked on plantations and farms. This was unfortunate since food was scarce, especially for poor black people. The years of growing nothing but cotton and little else had ruined the soil.

Cotton plants used up minerals in large amounts, draining the soil of nutrients. Even a good cotton crop was now hard to grow. This one-crop system bothered Professor Carver. He felt he must help the farmers find crops to grow in place of cotton, such as green vegetables. Vegetables would not leave the soil a wasteland after harvesting. However, it was not easy to make farmers believe that other crops would serve them better.

Carver wanted a plant that would grow well in poor soil and at the same time add nutriment to the soil. The peanut plant was his choice. The roots of this plant have small swellings. Bacteria that live in the swellings, called nodules, can take nitrogen from the air and make it useful to plants. When these roots are plowed into the soil after harvesting, they enrich it with nitrogen substances. Carver's science could not persuade the farmers to try peanuts. Although a few tried growing them, they quickly switched back to cotton.

Along came the boll weevil into the Alabama cotton fields. This beetle fed on the cotton plant and laid its eggs in the pods of cotton. The eggs of this beetle pest developed into larvae that fed on the fibers of young cotton. They began destroying acres upon acres of cotton as they had earlier in Texas, Louisiana, and Mississippi. The ruin brought on by the boll weevil forced the farmers to stop raising cotton, and they were ready to try peanuts as Professor Carver had been long recommending. (It is interesting to know that peanuts were brought to North America on slave ships during the 1700's. Slave traders used peanuts to feed the millions of people brought to America to work on the cotton plantations.)

The peanut harvest was large and the market small. More peanuts were grown than could be sold. Besides, peanuts from the Far East were being imported and sold in America for less money than American grown peanuts. Acres of peanuts rotted in the ground. Mr. Carver received much criticism. He faced a real dilemma. What could be done with all the surplus peanuts that he talked the farmers into growing in place of cotton?

THE PEANUT GOES TO THE LABORATORY

Being the scientist that he was, Professor Carver decided he would take the peanut apart. He wanted to know what it was made of. What would it be good for? He aimed to find new ways of making it serve his people.

In his lab Carver began to shell peanuts by the handful.

He saved the reddish skins and broken shells. The peanuts he ground into a fine powder, and heated them, and then put this peanut mash under a hand press. An oily substance dripped into a cup beneath the press. He then heated this oil at various temperatures to see what happened to it. The oil was also broken down into other substances, which he used to make soap, cooking oil, and rubbing oil for the skin.

By adding chemicals to the dried peanut cake that remained in the press, he extracted a substance vary similar to cow's milk, though it had less calcium than animal milk. From this milk he was able to make cheese.

Next, Carver removed the dried, crumbly peanut cake left in the press and placed it into a glass vessel. He added water and enzymes. The enzymes were substances that would help break down any proteins in the peanut. This mixture was placed in a warm water bath to activate the enzymes. By this technique, the different proteins making up the peanut were separated. He showed that a pound of peanuts contained just as much protein as a pound of beefsteak.

When he wasn't teaching his classes at Tuskegee, Professor Carver spent long hours separating the particles of matter that made up the peanut. He was taking the peanut apart chemically. This left him with simpler substances such as water, fats, oils, gums, resins, sugars, starches, pectoses, lysin, and amino acids. He then recombined them under different temperatures and pressures with other substances to make foods, medicines, and other basic materials. From the red peanut skins, Carver made a thin paper. From the shells which he saved, he made a soil conditioner and insulating board.

George Washington Carver (in black suit, center) is shown

As the years went by, Carver worked ceaselessly in the same laboratory room that Mr. Washington had given him in 1896. He kept adding to the list of products made from peanuts. By 1943, the year of his death, his investigations had led to the creation of over 300 products from

observing the progress of a student in the laboratory.

the peanut. And he also developed over 100 products
from the sweet potato, such as paste for postage stamps
and envelopes. And he produced colorful dyes and
paints from the clay in Alabama soils that could be used
in the home and in industry.

DR. CARVER'S LEGACY

For more than forty-six years at Tuskegee, Dr. Carver worked virtually alone and unaided. Unlike most scientists of today, he had no team of scientists or laboratory technicians to help him with his investigations. And it wasn't until 1935 that Austin Curtis, his only assistant, joined him at Tuskegee. Dr. Carver had very little money behind him. His laboratory equipment was never fancy or expensive. It was often crude. Much of it he made himself from discarded junk.

Dr. Carver showed that plant life was more than just food for animals and man. As you know, plants use sunlight as a source of energy to make complex substances such as sugars, fats, and proteins out of water, carbon dioxide, and minerals from the soil. Carver's first step was to analyze plant parts to find out what they were made of. He then combined these simpler isolated substances with other substances to create new products.

The branch of chemistry that studies and finds ways to use raw materials from farm products to make industrial products is called chemurgy. Dr. Carver was one of the first and greatest chemurgists of all time. Today the science of chemurgy is better known as the science of synthetics. Each day of our lives we depend on and use synthetic materials made from raw material. All his life Dr. Carver battled against the disposal of waste materials, and warned of the growing need to develop substitutes for the natural substances being used up by man.

Dr. Carver never cared about getting credit for the new products he created. He never tried to patent his discoveries or get wealthy from them. He turned down many offers to leave Tuskegee to become a rich scientist in private industry. Thomas Edison, inventor of the electric light, offered him a large sum of money to work with him. Henry Ford, of automobile fame, offered him a laboratory in Detroit to carry out food research. When the United States government made him a collaborator in the Mycology and Plant Disease Survey of the Department of Agriculture, he accepted the position with the understanding that he wouldn't have to leave Tuskegee. An authority on plant diseases—especially of the fungus variety—Dr. Carver sent hundreds of specimens to the United States Department of Agriculture.

At the peak of his career, Dr. Carver's fame and influence were known in every continent. People near and far wrote thousands of letters asking his opinion on scientific questions and seeking the privilege of working with him in his laboratory. Frequently, the professor from Tuskegee would not accept any money in return for the suggestions he gave and the various scientific problems he solved for industrial concerns and individuals around the world.

The peanut industry, in this country and around the world, is indebted to Dr. Carver for demonstrating the commercial possibilities of peanuts for many of the products on the world market today. The United States Department of Agriculture, through its Southern Utilization Research and Development Division in New Orleans, Louisiana, is still conducting research on peanuts, sweet potatoes, soybeans, and other vegetables. In its peanut products investigations, the substances in peanuts that give peanuts their flavor and aroma are being studied. Through chemical processes certainly more complicated than Dr. Carver used, new oils and protein substances have been found in peanuts and peanut flour. The food industries are interested in using these new substances for the development of new foods for the consumer market. Further processing of these new substances will make them useful as either animal or human food. UNICEF is interested in peanut products as a source of protein to feed the hungry peoples of the world where the supply of food with proper proteins is inadequate. Much research is underway to establish peanut flour as a high protein content food. One or two ounces of a protein powder from peanuts in a person's meal per day may be enough to raise the protein content to adequate levels to maintain health.

George Washington Carver, through his products, gave millions of dollars to the people of the South and the entire country. In a sense he is still giving and contributing to American life via the Carver Research Foundation at Tuskegee Institute in Alabama. A few years before his death he gave his entire life savings of $33,000 to establish the George Washington Carver Research Foundation for the perpetuation of his work in creative research. The purpose of the Foundation was to provide facilities and support for young black Americans engaged in scientific research. After Dr. Carver's death, the rest of his estate went to the Foundation, making his total contribution $68,000. Gifts of money poured in from friends of Dr. Carver and eventually a $2 million modern research building was erected for the study of agricultural chemistry, plant diseases, mycology, plant genetics, and agronomy. Over the years, hundreds of young men and women have studied and carried out advanced research at the Foundation. Giving these young gifted minds a chance to carry on research along the lines he had started was perhaps one of Dr. Carver's most important and meaningful contributions.

The Carver Research Foundation has made great progress in promoting research at Tuskegee Institute. Although work done in the area of chemurgy as such has not been done since Carver's death, large grants of money from government agencies have allowed the Foundation to move into broader and more modern areas of study. For many years the Foundation has been using isotopes (radioactive materials) as a tool for studying plant physiology. Cesium-137, an isotope, has been used by the Department of Food Technology to study the effects of ionizing radiation on perishable foods. The Foundation has studied the soil factors affecting the absorption of radioactive strontium by plants, the persistence of pesticides in soils, hormones responsible for the flowering and fruiting in plants and the feasibility of growing tea. This plant had never before been grown in Alabama soil. Such studies and many others that are extending the frontiers of knowledge in agricultural science all stem from the inspiration and humanitarian spirit of Dr. Carver.

Dr. Carver received many medals, citations, and honorary degrees for his achievements in creative scientific research and for his contributions to the improvement of health and living conditions of the people living in the South. In 1928, Simpson College awarded him the honorary degree of Doctor of Science. It was after this that he was called Dr. Carver. In 1939, he was awarded the Theodore Roosevelt Medal for distinguished service to science, and in 1941 the University of Rochester awarded him an honorary degree of Doctor of Science. The British made him a Fellow of the Royal Society. In 1948, the United States honored him with a three-cent postage stamp which included his picture.

On January 5, 1943, Dr. George Washington Carver died at Tuskegee Institute. He was buried on the campus near the grave of Booker T. Washington, Tuskegee's famous founder who brought Carver there. He never married, and left no known relatives. In January, 1945, the United States Congress gave national recognition of his birth by making his birthplace near Diamond Grove, Missouri, a national landmark.

Today, near the Tuskegee chapel and not far from the Booker T. Washington monument, stands a curved stone seat. Carved into a marble slab lying within its arc is this inscription:

GEORGE WASHINGTON CARVER
Died in Tuskegee, Alabama
January 5, 1943

A life that stood out as a gospel of self-sacrificing service. He could have added fortune to fame but caring for neither he found happiness and honor in being helpful to the world. The center of his world was the South where he was born into slavery some 79 years ago and where he did his work as a creative scientist.

GLOSSARY

Anomaly the angular distance of an orbiting planet from its point in orbit nearest the sun.

Aorta the main blood vessel that carries blood from the heart to all parts of the body, except the lungs.

Apogee the point in the moon's orbit farthest from Earth.

Astrology a pseudo-science that claims to know the influence of the stars and planets on persons and events.

Cell the basic unit of living matter of plants and animals.

Chemurgy a division of applied chemistry that is concerned with the industrial use of substances from farm products.

Constellation a group of stars.

Cross-fertilization fertilization of the egg in a flower of one plant by the pollen grain (sperm) from the flower of a closely related plant.

Egg a female reproductive cell

Ectoplasm the outer portion or layer of substance in a living cell.

Electrode a conductor, usually a thin metal strip, through which an electric current enters or leaves.

Electrocardiograph a device that detects and records electrical impulses from a beating heart.

Embryo an animal or plant in the very early stages of its development into a multicellular living thing.

Enzyme a chemical substance produced in living cells that can cause changes in other substances within a cell, without being changed itself.

Fertilization the joining of a sperm cell with an egg cell.

Floe a field or sheet of floating ice.

Fungus a type of non-green plant.

Hypertonic a water solution that contains more of a dissolved solid (such as salt or sugar) than it naturally does, is called a hypertonic solution.

Larva an early stage in the development of some animals that show a change in structure during their life development.

Latitude the distance north or south of the equator, measured in degrees.

Node the points at which the moon's path crosses the sun's path, as seen from the Earth, are nodes. (It is only when the moon reaches one of its nodes at a time when the sun is also at or near that point, that an eclipse is possible.) When the moon crosses the path of the sun from south to north, the node is called the ascending node.

Parthenogenesis a type of reproduction in which an egg cell develops into an embryo without being fertilized by a sperm cell.

Pericardium the sac-like membrane that surrounds the heart.

Plasma the liquid portion of the blood that does not contain blood cells or other solids.

Propagation the breeding of plants and animals

Protein one of the substances containing nitrogen which is a necessary part of the cells of animals and plants. Meat, milk, and cheese contain proteins.

Sextant an instrument used in measuring angles. In determining latitude, a navigator uses a sextant to measure the altitude of the sun.

Sperm the male reproductive cell.

Transfusion transferring blood from one person to another.

ACKNOWLEDGEMENTS

Illustrations and quotations are reproduced courtesy of the following institutions:

Illustrations

page 10:	courtesy of Howard University
page 26:	courtesy of the Provident Hospital and Training School
page 44:	Johnson Publishing Company, Inc.
page 49:	Schomburg Collection from The New York Public Library
pages 50, 61:	Boston Public Library
pages 68, 80:	"Transactions of the Academy of Science of St. Louis," Vol. XXIV, No. 9, December, 1923, plates IX and X
page 92:	Marine Biological Laboratory, Woods Hole, Massachusetts
page 116:	Monkmeyer Press Photo Service
pages 134–135:	The Explorers Club

Quotations

pages 47–48:	letter from James McHenry, adapted from *Banneker's Pennsylvania, Delaware, Maryland, and Virginia Almanac*

and Ephemeris, For the Year of Our Lord, 1792, Baltimore, 1791, pp. 2–4

pages 71–72: reprinted from *The Animal Mind*, by Margaret Floy Washburn, 1917, by permission of Vassar College

pages 76–78: the author is indebted to Miss Julia Davis of St. Louis, Missouri, for allowing him to study her personal notebook containing notes taken when she was a student of Dr. Turner's at Sumner High School in 1909

pages 89–91: A. G. Polman: *Charles Henry Turner, An Appreciation*, reprinted from "Transactions of the Academy of Science of St. Louis," Vol. XXIV, No. 9, December, 1923

pages 108–110: Just, Ernest, *Basic Methods of Experiments On Eggs For Marine Animals*, Blakiston & Sons, 1939, reprinted by permission of McGraw-Hill Book Co.

INDEX